Annamaria Giusti

Pietre Dure
and the Art of Florentine Inlay

With over 220 colour illustrations

For Silvano
Non satis est ullo tempore
longus amor

Translated from the Italian by Fabio Barry

Any copy of this book issued by the publisher as a paperback is sold subject to the condition that it shall not by way of trade or otherwise be lent, resold, hired out or otherwise circulated without the publisher's prior consent in any form of binding or cover other than that in which it is published and without a similar condition including these words being imposed on a subsequent purchaser.

This edition first published in the United Kingdom in 2006 by
Thames & Hudson Ltd, 181A High Holborn, London WC1V 7QX

www.thamesandhudson.com

Original edition © 2005 Citadelles & Mazenod, Paris
This edition © 2006 Thames & Hudson Ltd, London

All Rights Reserved. No part of this publication may be reproduced or transmitted in any form or by any means, electronic or mechanical, including photocopy, recording or any other information storage and retrieval system, without prior permission in writing from the publisher.

British Library Cataloguing-in-Publication Data
A catalogue record for this book is available from the British Library

ISBN-13: 978-0-500-51297-5
ISBN-10: 0-500-51297-3

Printed and bound in Spain

I. Detail of an ebony cabinet in the style of Louis XVI, c. 1765–70, by Joseph Baumhauer, with seventeenth-century Florentine mosaic. Chateaux de Versailles et de Trianon

II. Detail of a table in *pietre dure*, with floral and bird motifs, Naples, 1749–63. Madrid, Museo del Prado

III. Detail of an altar panel, realized in marble and *pietre dure* by the Corbarelli workshop, first decades of the eighteenth century. Brescia, Santa Maria delle Grazie

Contents

Chapter 1
The Ancient Splendour of Coloured Stones 9

Chapter 2
The Rebirth of Polychrome Inlay
in the Roman Renaissance 21

Chapter 3
Medicean Production in Florence 47

Chapter 4
The Fortunes of Hardstone Inlay
in Seventeenth-Century Europe 109

Chapter 5
Splendours of the *Ancien Régime* 159

Chapter 6
From Court Display to Bourgeois Luxury 213

Chapter 7
How a Florentine Mosaic is Born 253

Bibliography 258
Index 262
Picture Credits 264

CHAPTER 1

The Ancient Splendour of Coloured Stones

If forced to select one of the many studies (often true literary masterpieces) dedicated to stones, I would favour the dryly efficient work of the Florentine Agostino del Riccio, who in 1597 dedicated his *Istoria delle Pietre* (Gnoli-Sironi 1996) to all enthusiasts of 'beautiful and useful stones'.

It was just these qualities that must have appealed to our forebears in distant prehistory, and usefulness must have come first among them since, when hard, siliceous pebbles were sharpened or thinned, they became indispensable tools for survival, hunting, killing and cutting. When smoothed with other stones or abrasive sand, however, the stones gathered from the land lost their opacity and roughness to reveal shimmering and shifting colours beneath their polished surfaces. This brought to light the beauty of the stones, and their aesthetic appeal has never faded. They also seemed to embody other magical, religious and symbolic values that were not always or necessarily distinct.

Rarely, both in prehistory and the first millennia of civilization, were these beautiful 'jewels' regarded exclusively as ornamentation; instead they bore a magical and ritual significance that was diverse but shared by many civilizations and historical epochs. The tradition survives uninterrupted in the form of charms and amulets, as we may recall from the continuing custom of wearing good-luck stones connected with zodiac signs.

While the Palace of Menelaus evoked by Homer had walls of amber, and in the Bible, gold and ivory were the materials that roused the fantasy of the Psalmists, the Book of Revelations chose hardstones for the blazing vision of a heavenly Jerusalem whose splendour was 'like unto a stone most precious, even like a jasper stone, clear as crystal'. And to form the twelve foundations of the walls the Evangelist called into competition jasper, sapphire, chalcedony, sardonyx, beryl, chrysoprase and more – in sum total the entire catalogue of precious stones that were known and admired by the culture of the times. St John was writing in the first century AD, at a time when the reputation of precious stones had already firmly established itself throughout all those regions that had been touched by Hellenistic civilization, a civilization which had made the glyptic arts one of the most privileged manifestations of its refined artistic knowledge.

The very term 'glyptic', whose variants in many European languages all indicate the art of working hardstones, derives from the Greek *glyphein*, 'to incise'. This fact again confirms that it was the Greek world that laid the foundations for a tradition that would persevere through the coming millennia. It was also the reason why Hellenistic intaglios and cameos would become the archetypes of perfect beauty, models for the various 'renaissances' in the history of Western and Byzantine art.

In this, as in all the countless artistic genres practised in the Hellenic world, the passage of glyptic art into Roman civilization was a direct and happy one, partly thanks to the activity of much sought-after Greek craftsmen in Rome itself. As early as the Republican period (c. 510–31 BC), though primarily in the imperial epoch (31 BC–AD 476), engraved gems and cameos (Giuliano 1989) acquired a prodigious popularity amongst the moneyed classes. Their production extended from grandiose imperial cameos (ill. 3), monumental and celebratory jewels of power, to dense production of minute intaglios, engraved gems and cameos, which became an inexhaustible supply for the passionate antique collectors of the future, as well as the models of artistic inspiration.

1. Pavement inlaid with white, green and red marbles, designed by Michelozzo towards 1459. Florence, Chapel of the Palazzo Medici Riccardi

2

In the Roman world rare stones were not only the raw materials of exquisite carving, but also became a dominant feature of private and public architecture, which was sumptuously clad with the polychrome marbles that flowed into Rome from the ever-growing provinces of the Empire. In this case, yet again, Greek culture and the palaces of Hellenistic sovereigns – sheathed and paved in multicoloured marbles – provided the example. But it was in Rome that a type of decoration definitively concretized and took root, one that 'joined together' marble slabs to form geometric designs of chromatic contrast or more complex figurative designs: the type of stone mosaic known as *opus sectile*. This figurative art form, used for *sectilia pavimenta* (floor mosaics) and *incrustationes* (wall decorations) throughout the Roman world (Guidobaldi 2003), would enjoy a lasting and favourable future, which we will outline in the following chapters.

According to the exemplary testimony of Pliny the Elder (AD 23–79), elaborate marble pavements had already appeared in the age of Sulla, in the first decades of the first century BC, and became increasingly varied in style through the entire imperial period. Wall decorations, also based on combinations of coloured marbles, instead began to appear in the first century AD, in the Julio-Claudian era (ill. 4), and would reach an extraordinary refinement and complexity in the fourth century. The Basilica of Junius Bassus, whose inlays of mythological and circus themes were admired and drawn by Renaissance artists, or the Domus outside the Porta Marina at Ostia bear eloquent testimony to the sophisticated decorative style of late-antique *incrustationes*, as well as the role they would exercise over a millennium later in the rebirth of stone inlay in Cinquecento Rome.

The Christian buildings that began to rise during the same period in a Rome that was still imperial adopted the same artistic language as this world of marble inlays, aiming at a declared continuity of form in their renewal of meaning. So it is, for example, that in the Lateran Baptistery the acanthus spirals that had already figured in secular settings such as the *Domus delle Sette Sale* (*I marmi colorati…* 2002) acquired Christological overtones, as did the adjoining vases that allude to healing waters. It is, in fact, in palaeo-Christian cult buildings that wall *sectilia* would live out the last season of a great tradition that scarcely survived the downfall of the Roman Empire in the West. One of the last examples, from around the middle of the sixth century, is the Basilica of

3

2. Panel with a Dionysiac scene. Coloured marbles inlaid in a slate ground, from Pompeii. Naples, Museo Archeologico Nazionale

3. *Gemma Augustea*, cameo of first century AD. Vienna, Kunsthistorisches Museum

4. Pavement inlaid with marbles and glass paste. Pompeii, House of the Ephebus

4

5. Panel of bichrome inlay with decorations of Islamic derivation, in the pavement of the Florence Baptistery. First half of the thirteenth century. Florence, Baptistery of St John

6. East wall of the same baptistery, with cladding in white marble and serpentine from Prato

Euphrasius at Poreč, whose walls are encrusted with elegant geometries in diverse materials, including coloured stones, vitreous paste and mother of pearl (Terry 1986), and still followed compositional tastes that were established in Rome by the fourth century.

As was also true for other artistic genres that required special technical expertise and precious materials, after the demise of the antique world *opus sectile* declined in the West over the centuries, while it continued to be used in the Byzantine sphere. It was from Byzantium, in 1066–71, that the artisans arrived to execute, at the behest of Abbot Desiderius, the pavement of the abbey church of Montecassino, where *lithostrata* make their reappearance in the complex, ornamental 'carpets' of the paving, destroyed in the eighteenth century and known today only through engravings and the few fragments that survive. But in the marble arts of the time the pavement at Montecassino became the archetype for a tradition of marble inlay that would continue without interruption over the ensuing centuries, principally in the shape of those 'Cosmatesque mosaics' of Roman origins but widespread diffusion, and secondly in Tuscan marble inlay.

Cosmatesque mosaic, whose exponents extended far beyond the workshop of the Cosmati family from which it takes its name, became widespread from the twelfth to fourteenth centuries (Claussen 1989), arriving as far as England to decorate the royal tombs of Westminster. But its major area of dissemination was primarily central and southern Italy, where it sheathed floors and religious furniture. Ambones (pulpits), choir screens, Episcopal thrones and Paschal candelabra all bear polychrome inlays against a shimmering, white marble background, witnessing the confluence of Byzantine preciousness and 'classical' solemnity, qualities that are affirmed in the re-employment of rare, antique stones like red porphyry and green serpentine. The former came from distant quarries in the Egyptian desert, the latter from the heights around Sparta. Both porphyry and serpentine were emblematic of imperial Rome, which had loved them dearly, and when harmoniously set alongside white or subtly toned, yellow marble allowed early Cosmatesque mosaic to enjoy chromatic contrasts of severe beauty. Before too long these materials were joined by the scintillating gold of vitreous tesserae and the delicate colours of polychrome enamels, both of which enhanced the harmony of the marbles and which Arnolfo di Cambio (c. 1245–1302) would introduce to Florence, on the façade of Santa Maria del Fiore, at the end of the thirteenth century.

However, in Florence and Tuscany, where Cosmatesque had already arrived, the privileged form of mosaic remained bichromatic inlays, in white marble and the green variety from Prato (ills. 5 & 6) – the latter probably esteemed for its resemblance to antique serpentine. Such inlays articulate the rigorous architecture of the Florentine Baptistery and those other Romanesque churches that followed its model. Tuscan marble inlay, which also appears in Pisa from at least the eleventh century and with a third, red stone added, was initially aniconic and geometricized. However, from the thirteenth century on, it began to acquire figural motifs, particularly zoomorphic designs, which find complex and fascinating expression in the pavements of San Miniato al Monte in Florence, of 1202, as well as the floor that follows suit in the aforementioned Baptistery (Giusti 1994).

Although the West had, therefore, recovered the taste and means to create architecture in coloured stone, albeit with

7

8

7. Cup of the Ptolomies, sardonyx. Alexandrian artist, first century BC/AD. Paris, Bibliothèque Nationale de France

8. Vase in rock crystal engraved with hunting scenes. Saracchi workshop, c. 1580. Florence, Museo degli Argenti

limited materials and sombre harmonies if compared with the pageant of marbles in ancient Rome, much slower was any return to the working of gems, even if their appeal had never lost its sparkle. Just as High Medieval architecture had often drawn on the inexhaustible supplies of marbles amongst the ruins, for purely practical as much as symbolic reasons, so did goldsmiths reuse antique intaglios and cameos. The motivations for their reuse ranged from the intrinsic beauty of the stone and its finish, to the conscious 'appropriation' of and continuity with the antique world in which the gem originated, along with the magical-religious values that the stones bore from an antiquity even more remote than the classical world.

The extravagant cross of the Longobard king Desiderius is an example par excellence of the use of antique cameos on a liturgical object, following a practice widespread before the eleventh century and beyond, when the art of carving hardstones had been lost. The only exception was the brief but intense Carolingian Renaissance. In this period, within a general revival of the forms and techniques of the Roman world, artists showed themselves capable of executing portraits of emperors, dignitaries or religious subjects in rock crystal, a stone highly favoured throughout the Middle Ages for its adamantine purity, symbolic of divine light. Yet not even Carolingian artisans could succeed in resuscitating the other great manifestation of antique glyptic art, vase-carving, which would revive in the West only in the late Middle Ages, in simplified form and restricted areas.

Antique hardstone vases do nonetheless appear in the treasuries of the great abbeys and cathedrals, occasionally encrusted in sacred mountings that conferred still greater preciousness, just they did to various gems and cameos. A good example is the oval agate plate, of great refinement despite the sobriety of its forms and decoration, attributable to an Eastern workshop between the sixth and seventh centuries. It was once mounted on a Gospel bookbinding donated by the emperor Henry II to the cathedral at Bamberg at the beginning of the eleventh century. The treasury of the royal abbey of Saint Denis, in France, also vaunted amongst its wonders a sardonyx goblet that had belonged to the Ptolemies in Egypt (ill. 7), a fine example of that Alexandrine production so distinguished for its vase-carving during the Hellenistic period. So sophisticated were objects of this sort that perhaps their presence on French soil 'magically' instigated the revival of the thirteenth-century glyptic, whose strongest centre was, in fact, France (Hahnloser & Brugger-Koch 1985).

In 1292 the corporation of engravers in Paris included thirteen engravers of precious stones, fourteen of glass, and eighteen in rock crystal. Indeed, several vases, perfect in form and of the purest luminosity, from the first half of the fourteenth century, bear witness to the excellence of Parisian

9. *Madonna and Child*, carving in chalcedony and ivory with applied gems, pearls and gold. Parisian artists, end of the fourteenth century. Burgos, Cathedral Treasury

workmanship (*Die Kunst...* 2002). An older work of the second half of the thirteenth century may also be Parisian, a cameo of sardonyx (*ibidem*) that exploits the nuances of the stone in the most astounding manner. It juxtaposes the absolutely classical head of a young girl with that of a youth with an Apollonian profile, but dressed in the sort of 'civilian' cap fashionable in thirteenth-century cities. The other centre in which this cameo might have originated was Venice, which in the thirteenth century vaunted a corporation of master 'cristalleri' expert in the carving of rock crystal, and engaged primarily in the production of cross-reliquaries which enjoyed vast European diffusion. The diptych of Andrew III of Hungary, of 1292–96, in which the rock crystal accompanies a large engraved jasper, may be recognized as a Venetian masterpiece of the period.

In Italy, Sicily had preceded Venice in the glyptic arts during the first half of the thirteenth century, at the time of the great classical renaissance promoted by Frederick II of Swabia, a renaissance that had achieved cameos capable of rivalling their antique models. It is not improbable that these Swabian artisans, for the successful outcome of their glyptic creations, could count (*Federico e la Sicilia...* 2000) on a mastery in working hardstones acquired in the previous century in vase-carving (*Die Kunst...* 2002). This was an artistic genre in which the Arabs, who were the previous masters of Sicily and whose artistic influence was still felt, had distinguished themselves. Furthermore, in hardstone production Sicily, throughout her territory, could also count on the presence of rich stocks of vibrantly and stridently coloured jaspers. These stones would later become the delight of sixteenth-century collectors and patrons, but medieval art had already esteemed and exploited them.

Another territory in Europe where more jaspers than stones flowered was Bohemia, which would in fact avail itself of this national treasure in the manufacture of inlays, under the rule of Rudolf II von Habsburg (1552–1612). But by the fourteenth century Prague, which belonged to the artistic circuit of flamboyant Gothic, had already dedicated herself to the working of hardstones, under the impetus of Charles IV of Bohemia (1316–78), who saw in them the possibility to fuse the cult of relics with a faith in the 'virtues' of stones. One of the emperor's most significant undertakings was the construction of a chapel, in Saint Vitus Cathedral in Prague, dedicated to St Wenceslas and intended for the remains of his saintly predecessor. Clad in 1363–67 with a high dado, it included more than thirteen hundred pieces of hardstone (ill. 10). One seems to enter a monumental object of jewelry, studded with large and irregularly cut gems, which almost seem to cast a spell on this sacred place and consecrate it with their brilliance. This extraordinary creation, probably devised by the chapel's designer Peter Parler (1330–99), remained apparently without influence in its day and long after, until the regal mausolea of the sixteenth century lined with hardstones, like the Cappella dei Principi in Florence and the funerary chapel of the Escorial in Spain. To the sensibilities of a modern visitor the stones of Prague seem to prefigure not so much the slightly frozen geometries of the Renaissance, but the almost barbaric sumptuousness that the stones would acquire by privileging their 'intrinsic' force in the *Grotta* that Frederick the Great (1712–86) dedicated to the natural world in the Neues Palais of Potsdam, between 1763 and 1769.

But returning to the exquisite, flamboyant Gothic, it is no surprise that one of its most elect centres, France, had also

10. Cladding in Bohemian jaspers, Chapel of St Wenceslas, 1363–67. Prague, Cathedral of Saint Vitus

11. Cabinet façade, with seventeenth-century panels in Florentine inlay. Potsdam, Neues Palais, Hall of the Hunt

fallen under the spell of precious stones. In the second half of the fourteenth century the inventories of the treasuries of the king and royal princes mention numerous hardstone vases. These included the celebrated Rubens (1577–1640) *vase*, which belonged to the Duke of Anjou at the end of the fourteenth century, and later to Charles V before it entered the collection of the famous painter in the seventeenth century. A magisterial carved agate of the fourth century AD, it is enveloped in vine tendrils that could have been conceived by Lalique.

Many of the numerous vases and objects in hardstones, particularly rock crystal, cited in the inventories of Philip the Bold (1245–85) and Jean de Berry (1340–1416) were objects of contemporary manufacture, like the so-called *Plate of the Head of John the Baptist* (Paris 1400, 2004), in reality a jasper 'godonné' cup, which today can be seen in its primitive and turned beauty. One may appreciate still better the extraordinary glyptic mastery of the artistic circle around the Valois in the *Madonna and Child* (ill. 9), now in the Cathedral of Burgos but executed at the end of the fourteenth century for Jean de Berry. Its rich craftsmanship, in which the black mantle that envelops the ivory Virgin is cut in chalcedony, folded to softly model the waves of solemn drapery, leads one to conclude that not even the 'virtuous Milanese masters' could have done better; they who, at the end of the sixteenth century, transplanted the glyptic arts to Medicean Florence, inaugurating a 'new' genre of small polychrome sculpture in hardstone.

In fifteenth-century Florence, various hardstone vases of French, Byzantine, Venetian and antique Roman manufacture also entered the prized collection of Piero the Gouty (c. 1416–69), inherited by Lorenzo the Magnificent (1449–92) (Scalini 1997). Yet, there was no enduring revival of the glyptic arts in cultivated and Humanist Florence, despite the brilliant

12. *Libyan Sibyl*. Pavement inlay in coloured marbles after a model by Guidoccio Cozzarelli, 1483. Siena, cathedral

13. Tomb slab of Cosimo the Elder, executed by Andrea del Verrocchio, 1465-67. Florence, Basilica di San Lorenzo

14. Replica of the Holy Sepulchre, in white marble and serpentine from Prato, to the design of Leon Battista Alberti, 1467. Florence, Rucellai Chapel

exceptions of Lorenzo Ghiberti (c. 1378-1455), who made several cameos now lost (perhaps influenced in some way by his ties to French art), and Giovanni delle Corniole, Lorenzo's favourite artisan. In the interim the fascination with coloured and shimmering stones also began to manifest itself in Florence outside the canonical ambience of the sumptuary arts. In the 1430s, Donatello (1386-1466) inserted a Sicilian jasper tondo in the classicist medallion at the feet of the *Cavalcanti Annunciation* (ill. 13), and in 1465-67 Andrea del Verrocchio (1435-88) composed arcanely geometrical paving over the tomb of Cosimo de' Medici the Elder (1389-1464), using 'classic' porphyry and serpentine.

If del Verrocchio's design and materials were new, the pavement inlay is reasonably typical of the revival of marble intarsia, whether paving or cladding, that fifteenth-century Florence adopted from its uninterrupted Romanesque-Gothic tradition, with its persistent taste for abstract geometries (ill. 1). Siena, not far from intellectual Florence, instead expressed her pictorial vocation with magisterial experimentation into the potential of polychrome intarsia to depict figurative subjects and narratives. The great project for the Duomo pavement, which began as early as the late thirteenth century according to sources, was already fully underway in the fourteenth century and continued with growing complexity and expertise into the fifteenth, only to be concluded in the mid-sixteenth (Santi 1982).

For the entire fourteenth century and beyond sculptors and marble-workers, following cartoons designed by major artists, gradually covered the nave and aisles with panels of allegorical and biblical subjects in a three-colour palette of white, black and red (analogous to the Tuscan tradition) and, from the fifteenth century, with further inserts in yellow, brown, pink and grey (ill. 12). The broadening palette corresponded to a growing complexity and 'pictorialism' in the design of the compositions, and was obtained by joining marble slabs cut to perfectly matching profiles, according to the technical rules of antique *opus sectile*, and then 'drawn in' with etched channels filled with dark stucco. In the early sixteenth century the technique used by the marble-workers on the pavement of Siena had become so refined in its cutting and inlay of minute pieces of stone that it presaged the eventual virtuosity of Florentine inlays from the end of the century. It is this latter history that will be the theme and *fil rouge* of our artistic itinerary among multicoloured stones.

CHAPTER 2

THE REBIRTH OF POLYCHROME INLAY IN THE ROMAN RENAISSANCE

In the long and fortunate history of polychrome marble inlay that traverses the millennia and diverse artistic cultures, imperial Rome must be recognized as an especially fertile node of evolution (*I marmi colorati...* 2002). Its practices would be the foundation from which the Cinquecento rebirth of marble inlay drew its inspiration, as would the subsequent, polyhedric incarnations of the medium in Italy and abroad.

Opus sectile – a type of mosaic composed from slabs of polychrome marbles, cut to profiles and set alongside each other according to their colour to form a unitary abstract or figural design – experienced its greatest flowering under the Roman Empire from the era of Augustus until the fifth century. It developed into two primary typologies: *sectilia pavimenta* (Guidobaldi 2003), or paving schemes, and *incrustationes*, or wall revetments. These typologies represented a sophisticated and luxurious artistic genre for two reasons: firstly, the cost of the raw materials, rare marbles from diverse quarters of the empire; secondly, because of the complex working entailed, including cutting (in Latin *secare*) the slabs with saws and dampened abrasives, according to flowing and often jagged profiles that must dovetail with their neighbouring slabs with extreme precision.

In his *Natural History*, Pliny the Elder, the declared enemy of all those luxuries rampant in first-century AD Rome, denounced the new fashion for intarsia, even blaming it for the demise of wall painting since the new painting in stone was preferred over this traditional decoration. '*Coepimus lapide pingere*' – we have begun to paint with stone – writes Pliny, the only antique author to give us first-hand information on *opus sectile*, which must have evolved considerably by his day to be able to compete with painting, bearing in mind that the earliest designs in marble inlay were the simple geometrical combinations of first-century BC pavements.

Naturally a great deal has been lost, above all *incrustationes*, and by the time the Renaissance turned an eager investigative eye to the models of antiquity much had already disappeared. However, many floors had survived the destruction of ancient Rome along with a few splendid examples of wall *crustae*, like the intarsia in the Basilica of Junius Bassus (ill. 16). The anonymous artisans of the fourth century AD had clad the superimposed registers of the internal walls of this basilica with panels depicting mythological scenes and circuses. They also followed the modes and principles of true pictorial decoration, achieving their effects by exploiting the natural colouration of the stones, cut into sections of specific shape and always perfectly joined. Only a few panels survive today, divided among the museums of Rome (see text in the magazine *Amici dei Musei di Roma*), but some fifteenth-century drawings by Giuliano da Sangallo (1445–1516) portray much

15. Roman tabletop from the end of the sixteenth century. The antique marbles, abstract ornaments and large central slab are typical of Roman inlays of this era. Los Angeles, J. P. Getty Museum

16. *Hylas and the Nymphs*, wall panel in *opus sectile* from the Basilica of Junius Bassus. Roman artists, fourth century AD. Rome, Museo di Palazzo Massimo

17

17. Tabletop with abstract ornaments, from the Medici collections. Rome or Florence, second half of the sixteenth century. Florence, Museo degli Argenti

18. Tabletop with geometric inlays of marble and hardstone, with one of the first appearances of the naturalistic theme of flowers, Florence, Grand Ducal workshops, end of the sixteenth/beginning of the seventeenth centuries. Florence, Museo degli Argenti

more intarsia still in place on the various superimposed registers of the walls. Whatever was lost before 1400, and after, had largely fallen victim to the habit of recycling precious, antique marbles for new works, following a practice that became common in the Renaissance but which had a long prehistory in Rome from the end of the Empire onwards.

In fact, the medieval Rome of a thousand churches had never forgotten those antique marble techniques, which had disappeared elsewhere. It was these techniques that 'trickled down' into Cosmatesque mosaic. In vogue from the twelfth century, Cosmatesque combined the antique techniques of both *opus sectile* and *tessellatum*. It also added heterogeneous materials like vitreous paste and ceramics to the repertoire of noble marbles culled from the ruins, though with an almost exclusive predilection for red, Egyptian porphyry and green, Greek serpentine, stones that represented the Roman Empire par excellence and from which impressive reliquaries were also cut.

Cosmatesque mosaic was destined for a long and fortunate history, and would not only compose paving but also encrust architectural and sculptural furnishings. From the twelfth century until the late fourteenth, Cosmatesque disseminated from its original and principal home in papal Rome into southern Italy and Tuscany. It was no coincidence that these regions also enjoyed direct links with the Byzantine provinces, themselves heirs to the ancient Eastern Empire and reservoirs of invention and precious materials. The proof is the colourful, stone garb which paved and clad the architecture of medieval Venice, a privileged intermediary between Byzantium and the West, and which ensured that the lagoon city displayed absolutely the richest reuse of rare and precious, antique and coloured stones.

Quattrocento Humanism, whose engine of greatest activity was Florence, was responsible for developing both a new awareness of the distance of the ancient world and also nurturing a nostalgia for it, an awareness unknown to earlier epochs, and one rich in new and vital promise on both cultural and artistic planes. At first, this promise focused primarily on the 'forms' of Roman statuary and architecture, only later to emulate and venerate the materials that had materialized the Antique. First amongst these was again red, imperial porphyry, a material that was as evocative in its appearance as it was hard to work and which therefore stimulated 'great minds', as Vasari writes (*Le Vite...* 1568) – meaning Leon Battista Alberti (1404–72) and Andrea del Verrocchio – to grapple with the technical difficulties that the ancients had overcome so brilliantly (Butters 1996).

Formerly, in fact, Cosmatesque techniques of treating porphyry had been limited to sawing it into slabs, sometimes of notable size but always two-dimensional. Michelozzo (c. 1396–1472) employed the same modus operandi in the arcane pavement geometries of the Palazzo Medici chapel (ill. 1), as did Alberti in the inscription lettering on the façade of S. Maria Novella in Florence, though these were cut to more flowing profiles than any Cosmatesque work. A further step into the plastic realm of this hard material was taken by Andrea del Verrocchio in his 'carved architecture' for the sarcophagus of Piero and Giovanni de' Medici in the Old Sacristy at San Lorenzo. In the early 1500s, the cameo and gem engraver Pier Maria Serbaldi da Pescia (c. 1455–c. 1520) applied the working techniques of the glyptic arts to carving porphyry, achieving small-scale sculptures in the round like the exquisite *Little Venus* in the Museo degli Argenti, Florence. Within a short time, the partiality of Cosimo, the first ruling Duke of the Medici family, to the symbolic and dynastic value of porphyry, which had been reserved exclusively for imperial use in Diocletianic Rome, meant that mid-Cinquecento Florentine sculptors would perfect techniques of carving monumental statuary in porphyry, and these then became the proud ornaments of Florentine piazzas and grand Medicean palaces.

18

19. The monumental Farnese Table, executed in Rome shortly after 1560 for Cardinal Alessandro Farnese, to the design of the architect Jacopo Vignola. New York, Metropolitan Museum of Art

Yet, by this period the spectacular material variety and palette of the coloured stones of imperial Rome had already sealed their triumph in the cult of antiquity, collecting circles and artistic practice (Palacios 1981 and 1983; Tuena 1989; Giusti 1992 and 2000; Di Castro 1994; Napoleone 2001). From at least the beginning of the sixteenth century Rome, the new engine of Renaissance art and culture, fed the enduring and spreading passion for all the rare and prized marbles continuously recuperated from the inexhaustible 'quarry' of the ancient city. For the entire century and beyond, collectors from half of Europe converged on the city in search of knowledge and acquisitions, enthralled by the fantastic variety of coloured stones, which they valued as both the happy creations of nature and venerable relics of the ancient world. The stones were so venerable – though certainly not untouchable – that it was their status as 'antiques' that ennobled the new creations in stone. Although innumerable marbles, reworked or otherwise, left Rome during this period for the most distant locations – and so many that the Popes felt it necessary to draft early conservation laws to limit the city's material impoverishment – the architecture and furnishings of the new *Urbs Roma* widely exploited that extraordinary range of stones, which had originally flowed into the city from the empire's most far-flung provinces.

The ingenious techniques of *opus sectile* were also recuperated from antiquity. Even though these techniques had fallen into obscurity, they reappeared towards the middle of the sixteenth century in new forms and practices skilfully adapted from the ancient models. In Rome, the new *opus sectile* found especially fertile ground to develop into a long marble-working tradition, as well as transform the city into a centre and catalyst for artists of all origins.

It is significant that amongst the first and most requested masters of *commesso*-work was the Frenchman Jean Meynard, called 'il Franciosino' (active 1552 to 1584), who frequented Michelangelo's (1475–1564) circle and was active at the papal court in the third quarter of the century (Tuena 1988). The term *commesso*, for its part, evidently alluded to the joining

together (*commettere*) of the various stone pieces, and in this epoch referred to the same mosaic technique that the Romans had called *opus sectile*.

In Rome *commesso*-work for architectural revetment or the sumptuous ceremonial objects developed hand in hand during the middle years of the century. Thus, in a letter of 1555 the Florentine Bartolommeo Ammannati (1511–92), who had paved the nymphaeum of Villa Giulia, the residence of Pope Julius III (1487–1555), with coloured marbles, remarked on the tables inside: that their carved supports and tabletops were of 'marbles...with a surrounding frieze of mixed marbles.'

This was a new typology in furnishing, one that would become very fashionable among the rich and cultured patrons of the time. The precocious example that Ammannati mentions must already have displayed an encircling frame of coloured marbles, typical of many Roman tables, but it stood out both for its unusually large dimensions (4 x 1.4 metres), which will be difficult to find repeated later, and its sculptural supports with their own polychrome inlays. Pius V had such a pedestal executed in Rome towards 1570 for the liturgical font in the church of Santa Croce at Bosco Marengo. But such supports were rare among the sumptuous tables of sixteenth-century Rome, some of which have retained their solemn pedestals in carved marble but are usually devoid of any inlay.

A central support with carved marble volutes can be detected in the rapid sketch, dated 1554, of Giovanni Colonna da Tivoli that represents a small table with a square, inlaid top. An octagonal table standing on a white marble baluster, and still preserved in the Palazzo Farnese in Rome, belongs to the same genre. The inventories of the Palace list tables in rare marbles in 1568, and by 1653 they amounted to more than twenty-five items. Today some tables of noteworthy magnificence remain (Giusti 1992, Napoleone 2001), and may be ranked among the incunabula of a genre marked for success. For example, a square tabletop with rich adornments outlined by heavy white borders, and alternating *peltae* and roundels derived from the decorative lexicon of antiquity that inspired sixteenth-century Roman inlay, could also date back to the 1550s. Another constant of Roman tables, which already appears in this tabletop and the other Farnese slabs, was a dominant central slab of geometric form, cut from the rarest and most evocative slabs the inlayer could find in an already fascinating catalogue of antique stones.

Also from the Farnese collections comes the celebrated table today in the Metropolitan Museum of New York (ill. 19), executed in the 1560s for Cardinal Alessandro Farnese (Raggio 1960), whose arms are carved on the triple supports in white marble. On these rests the great rectangular, inlaid slab, of a refinement of invention and execution which shows how, even at such an early date, Roman inlay had arrived at a complexity unparalleled in contemporary architectonic intarsia, in spite of the fact that architects probably also designed tabletops. For example, the design of the Farnese table is attributed to Jacopo Vignola (1507–73), the Cardinal's trusted artist and designer of the family palace at Caprarola, where one may find pictorial decorations in an artistic key not dissimilar to the table intarsia. These tables are largely composed from rare, antique marbles, which form a frieze of cartouches and *peltae* encircling paired slabs of oriental alabaster. Only around this central 'window', as translucent and opalescent as a sheet of frozen water, in a subtle frame with minute corollas alternating with the heraldic lilies of the Farnese, appear the hardstones. In contrast to later Florentine practice, in Rome hardstones never predominated over the antique marbles favoured for such artefacts.

The other distinctive characteristic of Roman intarsia was the predilection for abstract designs, which, in the early stages of Roman production, apparently excluded figurative elements altogether. Their presence continued to be limited in the subsequent stages of Roman intarsia design towards the end of the century. Evidently it was a deliberate choice to select from the repertory of *opus sectile*, often extremely figurative, only those decorative motifs that were amenable to sixteenth-century architectural classicism, like the *peltae* on the Farnese tables, which were still used for the seventeenth-century pavement of the Confessio of St Peter's.

As regards the compositional and graphic aspects of the marble *commessi* of sixteenth-century Rome, the naturally 'aniconic' tendency of the architects who designed them must have been influential. Sensitive examiners of Roman antiquities such as the aforementioned Vignola and Giovanni Antonio Dosio (1553–c. 1609) were prominent amongst these designers in the early period, and this proved fundamental to the configuration of a repertoire of abstract-decorative themes that would remain in vogue for decades. The compositional schemes of the earliest Roman *commessi* could thus migrate, with an accentuation of decorative components perhaps requested by patrons, from architectural cladding to tabletops in stately homes, always sharing that abstract decorativism and knowledgeable selection from the repertoire of stones. This commonality is confirmed, for example, by comparing the revetment panels of the Sala Regia in the Vatican, executed under the pontificate of Pius IV (1559–65) with some of the oldest Roman *commesso* tabletops.

The Sala Regia was one of the first papal commissions to employ intarsiated marble revetment. In the course of the prolonged works to complete the room's decorations, lasting from 1537 to 1573, and from which emerged a 'multi-media' ensemble of sophisticated late-Mannerism, Pius IV had the lower register of the walls clad with a sequence of rectangular, *commesso* panels. Executed in antique marbles, they consist of two alternating modules, both of intricate design and centred on a great marble slab bordered by a frame with large ovals and *peltae*, outlined with white marble borders. A similar compositional attitude, with peremptory, white 'brows' underlining the coloured marbles, figure in the aforementioned Farnese tables, whose designs contrast with later examples in their simple and energetic constructionism.

The artisans of the panels in the Sala Regia were the Florentines Francesco di Barone and Ludovico da Fiesole, the latter also employed from 1567 on working the rare marbles dispatched by Pius V to furnish the aforementioned church of Santa Croce at Bosco Marengo, and perhaps identifiable with the 'Ludovico delle Tavole' who worked in Rome in 1564 for Cardinal Ricci, a Medici intimate. On the other hand, the ties between Florence and Rome in the field of *commesso*-work were from the first so close and diverse that it is difficult to distinguish the loans from the borrowings. The widespread presence of Florentine artisans and artists in Rome involved in *commesso* signified their engagement in a new genre, and perhaps also their superior technical ability. Conversely, in the 1570s Francesco de' Medici (1541–87), who could count on the continuing services of two inlay-artists that had worked for his father Cosimo, would summon to Florence the celebrated 'Franciosino', one of the most esteemed 'table masters' then active in Rome. Although the rulers of half of Europe fought for the services of Franciosino, he would eventually, in 1579, decide to return to his homeland and enter the service of Catherine de' Medici, Queen of France.

20. Tabletop in wood with inlays of jasper and ivory, executed before 1557 for Bindo Altoviti, to the design of Giorgio Vasari. Rome, Collection of the Banca di Roma

Although Florence did not enjoy precedence over Rome in the invention, or better still revival, of the art of inlay, she certainly became interested and involved at a very early point. The oldest document so far discovered concerning inlaid tables is Florentine, and refers to a 'square slab inlaid with various sorts of veined marbles', cited in the 1553 inventory of the furnishings of Palazzo Vecchio. Cosimo imported porphyry and veined marbles from Rome, as a 1559 export licence attests, among other things, by citing a slab 'of veined marble' (*ex lapide mixto*) destined for the Duke of Florence.

Moreover, various tables in the Palazzo Pitti were also of Roman manufacture, as Vasari records in a letter of 1567. It was, in fact, Giorgio Vasari (1511-74), the trusted artist and arbiter of taste in the Florentine court, who travelled often to Rome to supply and inform Cosimo I about stones and their artistic use, a subject to which he dedicated many pages. As early as 1557 Vasari had initiated his first project for an intarsia table for the Florentine Bindo Altoviti, a man of demanding tastes in artistic matters and whose portrait by Raphael still survives. Vasari would go on to make more tables for the Florentine aristocracy.

The Altoviti table, which Vasari himself describes as 'octagonal with jaspers set in ebony and ivory', can almost certainly be identified with the example now in the collection of the Banca di Roma (Palacios 1988; Giusti 1992). The decoration (ill. 20) is unusual, indeed so far unique, in the history of stone inlay. It takes the form of an arabesque that radiates out from a central knot in a complex pattern that remains brilliantly clear thanks to the chromatic contrasts between the ivory outlines, the Sicilian jasper inlays, and the wooden background. The perimeter band seems to echo the cartouche-and-roundel sequences of classical tradition, but here bizarre fantasy has made them Arabic in style. On the other hand, in the middle decades of the sixteenth century European art experienced one of the many 'Oriental revivals' to punctuate its history, and the motif of the arabesque enjoyed various applications and reinterpretations, for example in an environment tangential to Vasari, the Accademia Vinciana.

Nonetheless, the ivory fillets inset in the wood also suggest the direct inspiration of Islamic furniture, in which this dichromatic combination is widely used. Their recombination with hardstones reappears in an unpublished table-top in the Hermitage (ill. 21), which it is therefore tempting to attribute to a Florentine workshop from the second half of the sixteenth century, given Vasari's octagonal version, not to mention the dazzling display of large and small plaques in hardstones, jaspers, lapis lazuli, agate and vividly tinted amethysts. All of these stones evoke the 'jewels' in the two tables prepared in the 1560s, again to Vasari's design, for Francesco de' Medici, as well as the dominant passion of the heir to the Tuscan throne for such scintillating creations of nature.

According to Vasari's own account in the *Lives* of 1568, these two tables were executed by the Florentine Bernardino di Porfirio, the Medicis' trusted inlay-artist and craftsman of the Altoviti table. One table was 'of jewels with rich ornament' and the other, which is described at greater length, was 'a rare thing, all inlaid in oriental alabaster...with large pieces of jasper, heliotrope, cornelian, lapis and agate'. This description matches the shimmering display of the table now in St Petersburg, although in this case the backing is of wood, a combination not without precedent or analogy in Florence and not just on the Altoviti table. A table older still than Altoviti's is that in the Contini Bonacossi collection in Florence, in whose octagonal, nutwood counter are inlaid eight panels of precious marbles, and which must date to around 1550 given its very beautiful wooden pedestal carved with masks and lions paws (Giusti 1992). Another example that has been lost but which is cited in a Medici inventory of 1570 was a 'square table in nutwood inlaid with various sorts of stones'.

Wood was also the backing for hardstone plaques of intrinsic beauty employed by the great sponsor of decorative and figural inlay, Ferdinando I de' Medici. In the 1580s Ferdinando would employ inlay for the internal 'drawer' of the scenographic cabinet placed on the Tribune, which we know today only from documents (*Splendori di pietre dure...* 1988; *Magnificenza...* 1997) and from a few precious fragments.

Although hardstones became one of the focal points of Florentine artistic taste, dominating for three centuries the Grand Ducal workshop founded in 1588, this does not mean that they did not also make their presence felt in Rome in the second half of the sixteenth century, albeit slightly later than the great Florentine endeavour and either cladding regal and monumental furnishings or in the shape of small precious objects. In the first category one must include the monumental cabinet now in Stourhead House (ill. 22), Wiltshire, which oral tradition claims was owned by Sixtus V, and which should therefore date to his pontificate (1585-90) (Palacios 1981, I). It was purchased by the English noble Henry Hoare II during his Grand Tour of 1738-41 from a Roman convent, into whose hands it had passed from the last heir of Sixtus' family, the Peretti.

A dating in the pontificate of Sixtus V would perhaps be better confirmed by a close and exacting study, still lacking, of its bronzes and architectural details which overall correspond well to late sixteenth-century typologies, and whose structural and ornamental richness suggests a prestigious patron. Not only the façade but also the flanks of the three tiers and tympanum are densely encrusted with prize marbles and even more hardstones, chosen with an eye for vivid and dazzling colour contrast. Imaginative and subtle patterns combine the decorative modules of lapis lazuli, cornelians, agates, and oriental alabasters, almost evoking

21. Tabletop in wood, ivory and hardstones, probably Florentine and from the third quarter of the sixteenth century. St Petersburg, Hermitage

the changeable images of a kaleidoscope and always rigorously abstract.

The panels which vaunt more elaborate compositions, like those at the façade's heart and on the flanks of the upper tier, rework on a reduced scale the 'canonical' appearance of many Roman tables from the end of the sixteenth century, with a central oval slab framed by a frieze. Here this slab is also bordered by a collar of tiny hardstone medallions, following a successful decorative cliché that seems to mark all Roman production. In fact, we find it again in three shimmering tabletops made entirely from hardstones, probably in Rome in the same years as the papal cabinet. They resemble the latter in a preciousness that was singular even in an epoch of exquisite refinements like the late Renaissance; in the intense internal colour of the individual stones that dictated their combinations; and in the never repetitive and always inventive fantasy of the decorative modules, which everywhere respect the rule of 'non-figuration.'

Of these three tables, two of which are in a private collection (Palacios 1981, II; 1988; 2001), one must be of certain Roman provenance if it can be identified (Palacios 2001) with the great tabletop that reached Spain in 1587 as a gift to Philip II from the Cardinal Alessandrino, Michele Bonelli, so-called

22. Detail of the monumental cabinet, called the *Cabinet of Sixtus V*, made in Rome towards 1580-90. Wiltshire, Stourhead House

23. Reliquary aedicule in ebony, hardstones and silver, with the *Adoration of the Magi*, painted on a slab of amethyst quartz around the first half of the seventeenth century. Rome, private collection

because he hailed from Alessandria in Piedmont. Even though there are some discrepancies between the descriptions in old documents and the table today in the Prado, the Roman character of the latter appears incontrovertible, as is the regal quality of a work, which scatters hardstones over a surface measuring 130 x 255 centimetres. In the teeming, but never confused, decorative background with three central ovals, one notices hints of stylized naturalistic elements, such as the palmettes and short leafy shoots which also separate the geometric sequences of the encircling frieze in pairs. This 'concession' to figuration, absent in the sublime decorative abstractions of the other two tables, tends to confirm the table's Roman origin since it echoes the naturalistic decorations – here translated into minute hardstone inlay – that were gradually incorporated alongside the usual abstractions into a great many Roman tables made with antique marbles.

For the moment it is unknown which artistic ateliers in Rome engaged in such laborious and successful furnishings in hardstone, which required greater virtuosity than 'soft' marbles. These works must be attributed to the skills in cutting and setting of jewellers rather than marble workshops or stone carvers: men such as Curzio Vanni (Palacios 2001), for example, who was papal jeweller between 1599 and 1606 and who collaborated with Pompeo Targone (1575–c. 1603) at the end of the century on the Altar of the Most Holy Sacrament in the Lateran basilica, where a brilliant hardstone sheathing appears amongst the flickering bronzes. In 1600 the same artistic team joined forces on the tomb of St Cecilia, in the church by the same name, again using hardstones, a genre in which Pompeo Targone (an artist more famous than Vanni) must have benefited from apprenticeship to his father, a Venetian jeweller that had worked hardstones for illustrious patrons. It was again Targone who, in 1612, clad the four columns in lapis lazuli in the Chapel of Paul V in Santa Maria Maggiore, and his specialization is confirmed by one of the artistic biographers of the epoch, Giovanni Baglione (Baglione 1649), who writes that Targone was expert in metalwork, casting and working hardstones.

In 1600 a certain 'Maestro Donato' from the Abruzzi cut lapis lazuli for the Chapel of St Philip Neri in Santa Maria in Vallicella (ill. 25), begun in that year by the del Nero family and sheathed in intarsia dominated by antique marbles, according to Roman taste, while the ornaments that marry graphic vivacity with chromatic intensity were conceived and probably largely executed in Florence, the native city of both the dedicatory saint and the patrons (Tuena 1989; Giusti 2000). On the other hand, the artistic fervour of Rome and its employ-

24. Monumental tabletop in hardstones, of Roman manufacture from the end of the sixteenth century. Madrid, Museo del Prado

25. Detail of a wall decoration in polychrome stone inlay, in the Cappella di San Filippo Neri, around 1600. Rome, Church of Santa Maria in Vallicella

ment opportunities continued to attract artists from various parts of Italy, just as it had throughout the sixteenth century. In 1602 Pope Clement VIII conceded the Milanese Giacomo Antonio Cremona the exclusive rights to make intarsia in jewels and hardstones. Such inlays already enjoyed a solid and certified tradition in Rome: limiting oneself to only the most famous artisans, Valerio Belli of Vicenza (c. 1468–1546) had already lived and worked in Rome (Burns et al. 2000), a master in working extremely inflexible rock crystal. Giovanni Antonio de' Rossi (1517–after 1575) had transferred to Rome from Milan, a principal centre for glyptic arts from the Middle Ages, towards the middle of the century. It was to this artist that Cosimo I de' Medici turned for the famous onyx cameo, of 'imperial' dimensions and intentions, that portrayed the Duke of Florence with his wife Eleonora of Toledo (1522–62) and their children (*Splendori...* 1988).

Other Roman products, which were widely circulated in the first half of the sixteenth century and characterized by the use of hardstones, were the small aedicule-reliquaries often designed for private use, of wood but veneered with stone and painted, and which displayed a sacred subject in their inner frame. Many are preserved in public and private collections. Amongst the latter a representative example of the genre, and one that reflects canonical practice, is the aedicule from the Pallavicini collection (ill. 23), with a façade and tympanum in ebony, veneered with small hardstone slabs and ovals that frame an internal panel of quartz amethyst on which is painted an *Adoration of the Magi* in oils (*Splendori...* 1988). The creeping enthusiasm for beautiful stones, from late sixteenth-century beginnings to seventeenth-century diffusion, eventually led to a new pictorial genre that substituted stones for traditional supports. The artist exploited the natural markings as a naturally pictorial element with which to harmonize his artistic intervention. In the case of our small aedicules, the hardstone revetments encouraged and suggested the quite frequent choice of a central painting on a stone support.

Documents preserve the names of several artisans collaborating in Rome on these small but refined and delightful creations, whose ebony components were often entrusted to master woodworkers of Flemish origin, specialists in precious woods, as hard to work as they were durable. These included Remis Chilolz, who supplied the Pope with an object of the sort in 1636; Jean Cheller, Ranier Bruch and a certain 'Ermanno Fiammingo', who, in 1636, denounced the theft from his workshop of 'an ebony panel...with an ebony frame and varied stones depicting the Flight into Egypt and where the Madonna is an amethyst' (Palacios 2001). Even an established medallion-maker and goldsmith like the Lombard Gaspare Mola (c. 1567–1640), is recorded towards 1630 as crafting 'small paintings' in inlaid and painted hardstones for the major Roman families, including the Borghese and Barberini.

The internal painting was normally left to painters, who were attracted in numbers to the novel and fantastic genre of painting on stone, albeit some, like Annibale Carracci (1560-1609), only occasionally. However, there were several artists who became famous specialists in the genre, like the Frenchman Jacques Stella (1596-1657), also active in Rome between the third and fourth decades of the seventeenth century. Previously, from 1618 to 1622, Stella had worked in Florence at the court of Cosimo II (1609-21), where painting on stone was cultivated with energy and taste by many painters in the cosmopolitan circle around the Grand Duke, and where Stella could have acquired familiarity with this genre (*Bizzarrie...* 2000) (ill. 26).

But let us return to our principal subject, polychrome intarsia, and to the exquisitely Roman tradition that most amply represents it. For the entire sixteenth century, and even beyond, the inlays destined to dress architecture or tabletops 'for show' privileged antique marbles, inlaid and composed to form abstract decorations that were conceived to highlight the stone's value rather than the inventiveness of the design. One may perhaps notice in this a certain conditioning exercised by architecture on inlaid furniture. Nonetheless, after the initial period, furniture did relax its bonds with the models of architectural intarsia, which remained faithful to the sober and geometricized design that was employed in papal commissions of great importance.

Amongst these, the Cappella Gregoriana in St Peter's, commissioned by Gregory XIII (1572-85) and realized by Giacomo della Porta (c. 1540-1602) from 1572 to 1583, seemed to contemporaries 'the richest in varied marbles and the most ornate that has been seen until now', as the Florentine connoisseur Agostino del Riccio writes in his *Istoria delle pietre* of 1597 (Gnoli-Sironi 1996). The overall effect was that of a controlled and severe magnificence, perfectly in line with Counter-reform artistic criteria, which sprang from both the limpid geometries of the wall revetment and the chromatic harmony of the marbles, which exhibit a generally pale and slightly faded tonality. The only concession to a more vivid colourism, and to the figurative possibilities of intarsia, is the papal coat of arms at the centre of the pavement, the prototype feature that would mark subsequent papal projects.

Amongst these, in 1597 the Cappella Clementina in the same basilica reproposed with few deviations the model of the Cappella Gregoriana. This chapel, also by Giacomo della Porta, inclines to the same subdued colourism and sober marble frameworks, which seem untouched by the novelties of the previous decade. In 1585, works began on the Cappella Sistina in S. Maria Maggiore, at the behest of Sixtus V (1585-90), and concluded in the following decade. Within this vast scenographic ambience, the counterpoint of precious marbles from the Septizodium that Sixtus had demolished vibrate more warmly, modulated by the decorative preponderance of the inlays. Organized in long vertical bands, they present novel figurative inlays of the heraldic star and hills of Sixtus V Peretti's family arms, alternating with the usual abstract ornaments which also contain more complex profiles than ever before.

The author of the project was Domenico Fontana (1543-1607), aided by the young Carlo Maderno (1556-1629). After leaving Fontana's employ, Maderno would fulfil his personal inclination towards a more pictorial and decorative conception of revetment inlay, which becomes apparent towards the century's close in the Cappella Caetani in Santa Pudenziana. Francesco da Volterra (d. 1588) had articulated the chapel with wall divisions of classical linearity, but when Maderno took command of the project he enriched the scheme with plastic and intarsia decorations of a figurative character. Amongst them, for the first time, figure large vases that recall, perhaps intentionally, the monumental silhouettes of hardstone vases being produced in those years in Florence for the rising Cappella dei Principi.

Maderno's fame as an architect and his taste for marble colouration were 'consecrated' in the important commissions of Clement VIII (1592-1605). The most significant work of the Aldobrandini pontificate, much more than the Cappella Clementina, which, as has been said, reflected the slightly old-fashioned taste of Della Porta, was the renovation of the transept (or *nave clementina*) of St John in Lateran for the Jubilee, and constructed between 1597 and 1601. Above all, the aforementioned Altar of the Sacrament here concentrates a varied display of figurative inlays, which mix the emblems of the Passion with the Aldobrandini arms. Another important papal commission tied to marble inlay was the Sala Clementina in the Vatican Palace, of 1599-1602. Although modelled on the compositional scheme of the Sala Regia, the marble panels become still more evident, alternating inlays of the papal arms with amplified ornamental abstractions, which constitute the best precedent for the later cladding of the Confessio of St Peter's.

The shimmering revetment of marbles and inlays chosen to sheathe the Confessio of St Peter's (Giusti 2000), or burial place of the first apostle and pope, and therefore one of the most holy places in Christendom, forms a marvellous conclusion to the development of polychrome architectural inlays in the Roman renaissance. The Confessio was executed under the direction of Carlo Maderno in 1615-17, after a long design gestation that had begun in 1606 at the behest of Pope Paul V (1605-21), who not coincidentally came from the Borghese dynasty that had dedicated part of their lively artistic inclinations to precious stones. Paul V was the last great papal patron with a passion for works in precious stones – not only for cladding 'sacred' architecture but also, in harmony

26

with the eclectic collecting tastes he shared with his brother Scipione Borghese, as sophisticated furnishings. A table of this sort, which is today in the Galleria Borghese, comes from the family collections and represents a beautiful example of the Roman typology in vogue at the end of the century, with a classicized border of cartouches still following the model of Vignola and Dosio, enclosing a tangle of stylized floral patterns centred on the indispensable alabaster oval. It is also probable that in Florence in this period the Grand Ducal workshop of Ferdinando I (1587–1609) was preparing a table to donate to the Pope, and which perhaps remained incomplete given the isolated heraldic arms of Paul V in marbles and hardstones (Giusti 1978).

According to Baglione, the Borghese pope also satisfied his passion for precious furnishings by turning to Giovanni Fiammingo, known as Giovanni degli Studioli, 'who made cabinets in ebony, ivory, and some of intarsiated stones, which he fabricated with enormous industry.' Paul V transferred this taste for 'inlays of jewels' (*gioie commesse*) onto a monumental scale, which was likely incited by the contemporary project for the Cappella dei Principi in Florence, which was intended to be entirely clad with hardstones. The pope succeeded in beating the Medici, if not in magnificence at least in speed, for the Cappella Paolina in Santa Maria Maggiore was virtually finished in 1612. Designed by Flaminio Ponzio (c. 1560–1613), it could vaunt hardstone panels amongst its antique marbles, devoid of modish inlays but highlighted as elements of autonomous beauty.

In addition to the fascination of such a precious environment, intended to bewitch connoisseurs and commoners alike, symbolic values underlay this commission as they did many other similar papal commissions. The limpid and unchanging splendour of the rare stones configured the holy place *sub specie aeternitatis* as an image of Paradise. It is significant in this regard that seventeenth-century preachers extolled the Cappella Paolina as evoking the heavenly Jerusalem, whose gleaming architecture of hardstones is described in the Book of Revelations.

But to clad the Confessio of St Peter's, pope and architect returned to the rare marbles of late antique and palaeo-Christian tradition, orchestrated in broad and dazzling fields, or combined in intarsia with a strongly decorative impact, and which contributed a warm and embracing palette. The colouristic enrichment of the Confessio was without precedent even in Maderno's polychrome architecture, and was sympathetic to the architectural setting of the project, which exalted both the triumphalism of the Roman Church and the worldly grandeur of the Pope. The latter's arms loom large at the feet of the double stairs.

On an architectural level the Confessio concludes an essentially Roman tradition, but the chromatic continuum of its marble incrustations, and the unheralded prominence that *commessi* acquire there, seem to betray the influence of contemporary developments in monumental intarsia in Florence. This development was underway in the Cappella dei Principi, at the very beginning of a long process of construction that would span centuries in the years in which the Confessio was being constructed, yet already well known for its inlays which had been in preparation for at least twenty years. More typically Roman, and anticipating future develop-

26. *Jonah and the Whale*, painted in oils by Filippo Napoletano on a slab of 'lineato d'Arno', a type of *pietra albarese* found in the riverbed of the Arno. The border in polychrome marbles was made by the Grand Ducal workshops in the first quarter of the seventeenth century. Florence, Museo dell'Opificio delle Pietre Dure

ments in the city's inlays, are the Borghese heraldic emblems, the eagle and the dragon. They seem almost to have 'flown' the coat of arms to rest at the head and foot of the stairs, autonomous decorative motifs that at the same time glorify the patron's noble blazon. The dragon is an especially fantastic and dynamic variation on its heraldic prototype, with its agile and sparkling design, proto-baroque also in the immediate legibility of its broad fields of colour and free from the usual, late-Mannerist graphic subtleties and colourist refinements of the arms of Paul V.

The tabletops produced in the last three decades of the sixteenth century were as important as architecture in contributing to the fame and fortune of Roman inlay. Their production was, in fact, especially intense and skilful in this period, as far as one can glean from documents and the numerous examples that survive. They were executed by multiple craftsmen, and frequently they cannot be linked with any secure documentary reference (in contrast to the products of the Grand Ducal workshop in Florence, for which there exists a far greater number of documents). Yet their Roman origin can be deduced from the common characteristics of Roman tables from the late Renaissance.

We have already noted the unfailing presence of a central slab, more frequently oval but also in other, always geometric shapes (squares, rectangles, circles, polygons) that highlight an antique stone, chosen for its appealing colours. Often this panel was a piece of alabaster, a stone already much admired in ancient Rome, where it arrived primarily from North Africa and Asia Minor. The qualities esteemed were the variety of chromatic tones and nuances: *alabastro a pecorella* was sanguine and sparkling like clouds raked by sunset; *alabastro cotognino* offered rotating veining in sloping vortices with autumnal scales of colour; *alabastro fiorito* boasted mutating design and nuances. The range of choices for the decorations to encircle the central motif was also broad, and included any number of assorted, antique marbles, provided they were veined or mottled with vibrant and colourful markings: *verde antico, broccatello di Spagna, africano, bianco e nero d'Aquitania, semesanto* and so on (Gnoli 1988, 1989, 1996; Pensabene 1998; Napoleone 2001; *I marmi colorati...* 2002). Since Roman inlay did not pursue the figurative and pictorial predilections of Florence under Ferdinando I, choosing cuts of stone was principally dictated by the chromatic relationship that arose out of their juxtaposition, and artisans were therefore free from the meticulous search for the ideal nuance that was necessary for pictorial illusionism and which would intrigue Florentines so greatly.

As a result, as Roman inlays evolved from the sixteenth to seventeenth centuries, there is no noticeable variation in either the use of materials or the composition, which remained substantially faithful to tried and tested schemes: the central slab with inlaid border. We have already noted how in the initial phases the Roman decorative repertoire was limited to abstract ornament (ill. 28), involving various permutations of the prevalent, classicist motif of cartouches and *peltae*. But towards the century's closing the aniconic inlays began to accommodate figurative elements, alongside a similar development in architectural revetment, although independently, and more imaginative in their choice of subject matter. A favoured theme for tabletops was the military trophy, a theme again of classical derivation. Other recurrent themes were acanthus clusters, palmettes and corollas, which are always stylized in fin-de-siècle Roman intarsia and far from both antique naturalism and the 'proto-seicento' variety of contemporary Florentine mosaic.

Numerous tabletops belong to this genre, bearing witness to the quality and productivity of Roman workshops between the late sixteenth and early seventeenth centuries, a

27. Large tabletop from the beginning of the seventeenth century, in the Roman style and signed by Pietro Carli. Oxford, All Souls College

28. Tabletop with inlays in antique marbles, made in Rome in the last quarter of the seventeenth century. Liverpool, National Museum and Galleries on Merseyside

period in which the beautiful table of the Duke of Lerma, in the homonymous Collegiata at Burgos, may have been made. At its centre is an oval of rare *alabastro marino*, a stone that evoked the iridescence of the sea's surface at sunrise. Another oval, similar in its particular frame of concave segments, graces the centre of a table that once belonged to Cardinal Richelieu, in the Galérie d'Apollon at the Louvre. It is most likely older, as one may deduce from the predominance of abstract decorations throughout the overall composition (Palacios 1981, I). We have already remarked how even the most beautiful Roman tables were based on an almost constant repertoire, which often meant, even in the same workshop, reusing the same model for more than one work, with few design variations although differing palettes. This is the case for the aforementioned Burgos table, which finds a close relative in a table sold at Christie's several years ago, which differs only in the materials and frame of the central oval as well as certain details of the bordering frieze.

Another beautiful example of the possible combinations of panoplies, *peltae*, floral patterns and corollas, is a teeming tabletop at All Souls College, Oxford (Giusti 1992) (ill. 27). The cartouche that heraldically frames the oval of *alabastro fiorito*, and the four 'feathered', more naturalistic leaves that curve in on themselves, suggest a dating in the seventeenth century. Just to stir the already muddy waters of influence and counter-influence between Rome and Florence in the field of inlay, the *giallo antico* border of this typically Roman artfact bears the engraved signature 'M. PIETRO CARLI FIO[RENTINO] FECIT,' a craftsman whose name is so far only known from this inscription, and which is a rarity on inlays both from this period and later.

In some rare cases, currently limited to two tables in Madrid – one in the Prado and the other in the Museum of Decorative Arts (Palacios 2001) – the military panoplies acquire an unusual prominence and complexity in design. Indeed, in the larger and richer of the pair (ill. 29), in the Prado, dating from around 1600 and formerly the property of the powerful Duke of Lerma's favourite, Don Rodrigo Calderón, expressive figures of Turks appear yoked to cannons, a theme that must have been especially pleasing in Spain after the victory of Lepanto. Following this battle, Don Juan of Austria, admiral of the Christian fleet, had received an inlaid table as a papal gift (Tuena 1988, Palacios 2001), confirming that this type of artefact was prestigious and esteemed.

Ferdinando de' Medici was certainly among the first and most refined connoisseurs. As a younger son of Cosimo I, he was nominated Cardinal Deacon and, in this office, resided at length in Rome between 1563 and 1587, when he ascended to the throne of Tuscany on the death of his childless brother Francesco I. During this sojourn of over two decades, Ferdinando, in his privileged position of cardinal and representative of the Medici, found himself thoroughly at home in the sophisticated intellectual climate of this capital of the arts, the engine of that antiquarian passion for ancient marbles which had already enthralled Cosimo. But while Cosimo and Francesco maintained frequent and not always easy commerce with Rome in order to transfer materials, artefacts and artists there, Ferdinando could avail himself first-hand of the best local resources, to which he turned for the magnificent fittings of his villa and garden at Trinità dei Monti, acquired in 1575 (*Il sogno di un cardinale…* 1999). Amongst its furnishings were several inlaid tables.

Three of these were acquired by Florentine museums in 1789 and have remained in their collections to this day. The largest (ill. 30), in the Galleria Palatina, is perhaps also the oldest and was certainly made before 1588, when it is described in an inventory of the Villa Medici (Giusti 1979). Its monumental dimensions, which seem almost a constant in Cinquecento Roman tables destined for illustrious patrons but which would later diminish in size, and above all the composition of the tabletop, with its central oval and decoratively abstract frieze, belong to a typology of Roman tables from the third quarter of the sixteenth century. It does, however, vaunt some inventive details, like the unusual prominence of the central oval in *smeraldina di Spagna* (fluorite), whose concentric and parallel striations intermingle like a crystal rainbow to reveal nuances that range from dewy green to violet.

The overall design, including the tight concatenation of motifs in the frieze, displays the solemn cadence and limpid decorative articulation of an architectural revetment, so much so that it may be attributed to Giovanni Antonio Dosio (Morrogh 1985). Dosio probably executed some watercolours for tabletops now in the Uffizi and not dissimilar to the slabs in the Galleria Palatina. Furthermore, the inextricable ties between Roman intarsia and the Florentine debut of Dosio as an architect constituted an important *trait d'union*. Of Tuscan origins, Dosio was trained and worked in Rome, and contributed to the formulation of an architectural language in the middle decades of the sixteenth century. Having entered the orbit of Ferdinando de' Medici, as one must presume from the table now in the Palatina, he re-established his ties with Florence by designing the polychrome revetments of the Gaddi Chapel in Santa Maria Novella (1575–76) and the Niccolini Chapel in Santa Croce (1579–89), in which the dry architectural language of Florence finally absorbed the antiquarian influences of Rome.

Another table from Ferdinando de' Medici's Roman sojourn, which features his cardinal's arms on a very beautiful pedestal of carved and gilt wood, is now in the Museo degli Argenti (Giusti 1979, Palacios 2000). It is called the 'Table of the Zodiac' because in the encircling border it bears stylized zodiacal emblems inlaid in *nero del Belgio* within *lumachella* medallions. This subject matter, which was favoured in

29. Large tabletop, with motifs alluding to the Battle of Lepanto, Rome, c. 1600. Madrid, Museo del Prado

30. Large tabletop formerly in the Villa Medici in Rome, to a probable design by the architect Giovanni Antonio Dosio. Made in Rome in the third quarter of the sixteenth century. Florence, Galleria Palatina

medieval paving inlays but was unusual for a Cinquecento inlay, was not simply the pretext for decoration but probably alluded to the ties between the world of stones and the realm of the stars, a concept as ancient as human history and one that was given renewed impetus in the astrological and alchemical inclinations of mature Renaissance culture. Even the meticulously calculated geometrical relationships that connect the quadrants on the Table of the Zodiac, the circles and ellipses, seem to originate less in the taste for rigorous modules common to the oldest *commessi* than to delineate esoteric, astrological trajectories.

The most original (ill. 31) amongst these three unusual tables was previously in the Villa Medici but is now at Poggio Imperiale. It presents a central slab of *alabastro marino*, on whose sides, among rare and antique marbles in geometrical panels, inserts of transparent alabaster are painted with mythological subjects and grotesques in grisaille on their back surfaces (Giusti 1979; Palacios 2001). Although there are many examples of painted alabaster in the intarsia of the era of Ferdinando I, they are restricted to few inlays, and subordinated to, indeed overwhelmed by, the polychrome splendour of the stones around them. Instead, in the Poggio table, the designs below the alabaster, which betray the themes and brilliant artistic style of the post-Raphaelesque Roman ambience, find a figurative autonomy and opalescence which illuminate the wilfully subdued chromatic harmonies of the stones, in comparison with which they seem to occupy a 'background' of illusionist depth.

Undoubtedly Cardinal Medici had access to good artists in Rome, but the singular character of his tables within Roman inlay practice lead one to conclude that his personal tastes as a patron of the arts and 'beautiful stones' must have weighed on their design. This hypothesis finds confirmation in subsequent phases of Florentine *commesso* work, whose 'pictorial' character was imposed by Ferdinando, by then Grand Duke, and was never to be abandoned.

This was not, however, the route that Roman inlay would take. For the entire seventeenth century, Roman intarsia pursued without break the tried and tested typologies devised at the end of the previous century, combining abstract motifs with vegetal ornament – the latter gradually acquiring greater prominence – and more naturalistic accents in the compositional economy of tabletops. These tabletops were also still capable of displaying an assortment of antique marbles despite their increasing rarity and papal proscriptions on their quarrying. Often the traditional cartouches were concentrated in the table's central zone, in more amplified forms and with more dynamic design, while the border of foliate shoots and flowers simultaneously became more complex and spread sometimes to include small birds and snails, perhaps under the influence of contemporary Florentine production, and almost camouflaging them in the overall decorative tangle. Three great 'sister' tables correspond to this typology, in the Palazzo Ducale at Mantua, the Metropolitan Museum of New York and at Charlecote Park (Wiltshire), the latter coming from the Borghese collection in Rome (Giusti 1992; Palacios 2001), and all probably derived, with few variations, from a single cartoon according to a practice that, as we have noted, was usual in Roman workshops.

More original is instead the composition of vegetal motifs and animals that we find on a square table in the Doria Pamphili collection in Rome (Palacios 1981, I; Napoleone

31

31. Table formerly in the collection of Cardinal Ferdinando de' Medici, with prints under the alabaster and geometric inlays in antique marbles. Made in Rome in the third quarter of the sixteenth century. Florence, Villa del Poggio Imperiale

32. Detail of pavement in coloured stone inlays, 1696–97, in the Chapel of St Ignatius. Rome, church of the Gesù

2001). They appear not just in the frame, which is in itself beautiful, with its loose and vibrant acanthus spirals, but above all in the great central panel of alabaster, where real and imaginary aquatic fauna nest in the fleeting pools formed by the veins in the stone.

As far as architectural intarsia is concerned, an art form that we have seen was decisive in the birth and development of Roman inlay, its two-dimensional character did not recommend itself to the plastic tastes of baroque architecture which took root in the second decade of the Seicento. But intarsia was not abandoned altogether. Rather it was empowered and exalted by the Roman baroque, the triumphal and embracing colourism of antique and modern marbles, taking the shape of columns, pilasters, revetment and so on, which sensually highlighted their veining and colour combinations, as Gian Lorenzo Bernini (1598–1680) superbly accomplished in the Cornaro Chapel in Santa Maria della Vittoria, in 1649–53.

Decorative and figural intarsia continued to find application in architectural furnishings thanks to its two-dimensional nature: altar frontals, tomb slabs and paving, deploying a repertoire of floral triumphs, heraldic arms, sacred and funerary symbols, often routine but in most cases designed by prominent artists, Bernini among them. At the end of the century, in 1696–97, one of the happiest products of Roman inlay (ill. 32) was executed in the most important chapel of the church of the Gesù, dedicated to the founder, St Ignatius Loyola. Designed by Filippo Bay (Napoleone 2001), the floor has become a spreading carpet of shoots, leaves and flowers, of grandiose and vibrant design, exalted by the rich and warm palette of the many stones utilized.

Tied to the same style is one of the rare Roman tables from the second half of the century, and one fabricated for an illustrious destination. Today it may be found at Versailles, and was acquired in Rome for Louis XIV of France in 1685 (Giusti 1992). At the time the Gobelins factory produced high quality mosaics and mosaic reliefs for the Sun King, but he had not abandoned his youthful habit of acquiring Roman inlays, imparted to him by his mentor Cardinal Mazarin.

The fortunes of Roman intarsia, which had once been so crucial to the 'take-off' and dissemination of the genre, were by now declining but would experience a vigorous resurgence in the wake of Neoclassical taste and the consuming passion for antique marbles.

CHAPTER 3

Medicean Production in Florence

Although as the sixteenth century progressed, Florence gradually ceded its lead as Rome became the driving force behind the greatest artistic innovations, in the field of the applied arts it maintained and even revived a brilliant activity nurtured by the patronage of the Medici dynasty. In fact, in 1588 Ferdinando I de' Medici (r. 1587–1609), the third Grand Duke of Tuscany, became the first European sovereign to found a 'State' factory, in which eclectic workshops enjoyed the exclusive patronage of a court with sophisticated and demanding artistic tastes (ill. 33).

The Galleria dei Lavori created by Grand Duke Ferdinando I de' Medici, which became the model for similar royal workshops such as Louis XIV's (1638–1715) Gobelins manufacture, immediately acquired an international reputation, primarily for its refined hardstone creations. These became so recognized as a Florentine speciality that the Grand Ducal manufacture outlived the Medici dynasty (Zobi 1853; Rossi 1967; *Splendori...* 1988; Giusti 1992) and survives even to this day as the Opificio delle Pietre Dure, an institution that is still active and operational, although it now restores works of art rather than creating them.

Ferdinando I, who was able to unite his own artistic passions with a firm vocation as a State administrator, founded the workshop; but the pre-eminence that hardstone works immediately enjoyed and the extraordinary technical virtuosity (ill. 34) that distinguished them had already been fostered by the patronage and collecting of Ferdinando's father Cosimo I (1519–74), the first Grand Duke, as well as the brilliant experimentation of Cosimo's eldest son, Francesco I de' Medici (1541–87) (*Magnificenza...* 1997; Acidini Luchinat 1997).

The love of glyptic arts that had inspired Piero the Gouty and Lorenzo the Magnificent (Heikamp 1972) to assemble a princely collection of cameos and ancient and modern vases (ill. 36), was inherited by Cosimo I, who was caught up in the triumphant vogue for hardstone vases, favoured objects in Cinquecento collections. The rarefaction of the antique models available on the market, which could still be acquired with comparative ease in the fifteenth century, achieved its

33. Coat of arms of Ferdinando I de' Medici, inlaid in the hardstone pavement of the Chapel of the Virgin Annunciate. Grand Ducal workshops, early decades of the seventeenth century. Florence, Basilica of the Santissima Annunziata

34. Plaque with *View of the Piazza della Signoria*, in gold and hardstones, from the crown of the cabinet of Ferdinando I de' Medici, formerly in the Uffizi Tribuna, 1599–1600. Florence, Museo degli Argenti

35. Tabletop assembled by the Florence manufacture at the end of the eighteenth century, reusing two older panels with vases of flowers executed around 1610 for the unfinished altar of the Cappella dei Principi. The three classical-style, red-figure plaques in the central zone date to the eighteenth-century assembly. Paris, Musée du Louvre

acme in the Milanese workshops of hardstone engravers (Kris 1929; *Die Kunst der Steinschnitts* 2002). Even in the Middle Ages, this city had cultivated a tradition of engraving hardstones that was rare for the epoch, particularly transparent rock crystal that was often favoured for liturgical objects as a symbol of light and purity. It is therefore not surprising that during the Renaissance, Milanese and Lombard specialists were still capable of executing pieces that were worthy of ancient Rome in their technical expertise, but modelled on the more 'modern', unusual and metamorphic forms favoured by Mannerist taste.

The greatest specialists in their field, and suppliers to the greatest courts and collectors in Europe, were the ateliers of Saracchi, Annibale Fontana (1540–87) and Miseroni, on whom Cosimo called on more than one occasion. Vasari writes that 'one has seen most beautiful vases and goblets of crystal' made by the brothers Gasparo (1518–73) and Girolamo (1522–84) Miseroni (Distelberger 1983), mentioning in particular two pieces made for Cosimo that were even 'miraculous', as well as a large vase of lapis lazuli.

The diamantine clarity of rock crystal, which arrived in Milan from the neighbouring Gotthard, and the dazzling blue of Persian lapis were conspicuous in Cinquecento stone carving, even more than agate and chalcedony, despite the fact that the latter were ennobled by their use in the classical era. Lapis is used for a cup in the Museo di Mineralogia in Florence, in the form of a shell clasped by a sea monster and supported by a tortoise, a wax model for which

Gasparo Miseroni presented to Cosimo in 1563 for preliminary approval (*Die Kunst der Steinschnitt* 2002).

Although the hardstone vases in collections were almost entirely made from scratch, antique cameos and engraved gems were still being rediscovered or surfaced in new archaeological excavations. The Medici collection of antiquities, which was passed down to Cosimo I in rather modest form thanks to the dispersal it had suffered during the Medici exile from Florence, was enlarged by him and his consort Eleonora of Toledo, herself a passionate collector of antique gems and cameos (Tondo-Vanni 1990). The twelve superb cameos by different hands that decorate the flanks of a cabinet belonging to Cosimo I, a striking masterpiece of the goldsmith's and glyptic arts that has recently resurfaced in an English private collection, also seem to be of classical origin (*Magnificenza...* 1997). Yet, however many classical cameos were still in circulation, even greater was the number of able and highly rated craftsmen that attempted the genre, which had already thrived in the fifteenth century. In this field Florence also enjoyed its own tradition, which had flourished at the time of Lorenzo the Magnificent in the person of the famous Giovanni delle Corniole (*c.* 1470–after 1516) and persisted without interruption until Cosimo I. Cosimo availed himself of the local carver Domenico di Polo, who had trained with Pier Maria Serbaldi da Pescia, yet another artist already active under Lorenzo. Nonetheless, for more ambitious enterprises, like the great chalcedony cameo (ill. 37) in the Museo degli Argenti that represents Cosimo and his family and imitates

36

37

the imperial cameos of ancient Rome (*Splendori di pietre dure...* 1988), the Grand Duke preferred to turn to contemporary Rome and an artist of international repute like Giovanni Antonio de' Rossi (1517–post 1575).

We have already noted how Rome, the heart of artistic and antiquarian culture during the Renaissance, was also the point of reference for another, evocative application of precious stones, that of inlay or *commesso* conceived to imitate the *opus sectile* of ancient Rome, and composed of variegated marbles retrieved from ancient ruins and the recent excavations of imperial Rome (*I marmi colorati...* 2002).

Among the many antique-lovers and collectors that converged on Rome, Cosimo I de' Medici was one of the first to procure antique marbles and *commesso* tabletops, even though he also encouraged Florentine production in this area. Indeed, Cosimo reserved a laboratory space in his new Ducal residence at the Palazzo Vecchio for this activity, and here worked Bernardino di Porfirio da Leccio (doc. 1557–88), 'of the county of Florence', who crafted 'small tables...inlaid with jewels' to Vasari's design in the 1560s under the commission of Cosimo and his son, Prince Francesco (Vasari 1568 and 1967; Butters 2000).

It was, in fact, under Francesco de' Medici, as low-profile in government as he was brilliantly innovative in the arts (Berti 1967), that Florence acquired and consolidated its autonomy and originality in the decorative arts, particularly the working of precious stones. Francesco, just like Cosimo before him, became so personally enraptured by the artistic techniques involved that he learnt to practise them with a certain ability, and personally oversaw on a daily basis the birth of the *commesso* work and carving that would compete with Milanese and Roman production. Alongside hardstones, Francesco also sought to introduce to Florence some more unusual artistic techniques until then restricted to other cities, such as Venetian glass and Chinese porcelain (*Magnificenza...* 1997; Butters 2000; *L'ombra del genio...* 2002). In 1576 the Venetian ambassador observed to this effect, in one of his periodic reports to the Venetian government, that Francesco 'has devoted all his delight to certain arts, in which he makes a habit of finding and adding many innovations.' It was not, therefore, pure and simple technical imitation, however daring, but also the ambition to achieve new artistic expression, for which Francesco rightly counted on the brilliant marriage between the manual skill of the craftsmen and the tireless invention of the artists in his entourage. From the latter category emerged the sparkling imagination of Bernardo Buontalenti (1536–1608), the versatile *genius loci* of the Casino di San Marco.

36. Vase in jasper, of thirteenth-century Venetian manufacture, with fifteenth-century mountings in enamels and gilded silver, formerly in the collection of Lorenzo the Magnificent. Florence, Museo degli Argenti

37. Chalcedony cameo with portraits of Cosimo I de' Medici, Eleonora of Toledo and their children, carved in Rome by Giovanni Antonio de' Rossi, 1559–62. Florence, Museo degli Argenti

38. Flask of lapis lazuli carved in the Medici workshops to a design by Bernardo Buontalenti, with a mounting in gold and enamels by Jacques Bijlivert, 1581–84. Florence, Museo degli Argenti

38

39. Wooden tabletop with hardstone inlays and gilt bronze, formerly set within a late sixteenth-century cabinet, now lost. Florence, Museo di Mineralogia

40. Tabletop in hardstones, in a geometric style anticipating the inlays that would be made for Ferdinando I de' Medici, 1560–80. Florence, Museo degli Argenti

But it was in *pietra dura*, inlay and carving, that Francesco succeeded in establishing a field of artistic supremacy that Florence would maintain for centuries, sustained by a passion that the first Grand Dukes shared with equal intensity and transmitted to their descendants. Francesco's interest in alchemy and science and his inventive artistic tastes impelled him to privilege not so much the antique marbles venerated by Cinquecento classicism, but the magical and inexhaustible supply of hardstones in which nature seemed to have given rein to her greatest flights of fantasy. Moreover, what gave added value to the intrinsic beauty of the stones was the 'ingenious artifice' needed to bend siliceous materials to artistic invention, while their durability further guaranteed their perpetual splendour. It is no coincidence that Francesco dreamed of cladding the dynastic mausoleum of the Medici, which he was never able to begin but which he planned to perpetuate the memory of the ruling family, with 'precious stones, Chalcedonies, Prases, Sardonyxes, Agates and Jaspers, of varied colours, all gathered by him with due industry, and already planned for this use...' as the eulogy intoned at his funeral. The sacred place of death would have been sheathed with the most durable products that nature offered, and would have perpetuated in time the memory and magnificence of the Medici.

Not only did Francesco de' Medici dedicate himself to collecting evocative stone samples, but his demands exceeded the capacities of the few local carvers who had worked for his father. Nor did he restrict himself to his collection of vases, however splendid, which were conceived and executed elsewhere. He decided to import to Florence the technical excellence of the Milanese craftsmen. In 1572 the Milanese brothers Ambrogio (d. 1606) and Stefano Caroni (d. 1599) – all well-known hardstone carvers – moved there permanently, attracted to Florence by the generous salary that Francesco offered. In 1575 they were followed by Giorgio Gaffurri (d. 1591), also Milanese and the head of a family workshop, who like the others was now lodged at the Casino di San Marco. The latter was completed in 1574 and Francesco planned it as the seat of his artistic and scientific workshops, anticipating the Galleria dei Lavori that would be inaugurated at the end of

41

41. Heraldic arms of one of the cities of the Grand Duchy of Tuscany, in preparation at the end of the sixteenth century for the cladding of the Medici mausoleum. Florence, Cappella dei Principi

42. Interior of the Cappella dei Principi, founded in 1604 and completed in the middle of the nineteenth century. Florence, Cappella dei Principi

43. Detail of the altar *paliotto*, with inlays suggesting an embroidered altar cloth, executed between the end of the sixteenth and the beginning of the seventeenth centuries to the design of Jacopo Ligozzi. Florence, church of the Ognissanti

the subsequent decade. It is again one of the detailed reports of the Venetian ambassador that gives the most effective description of the Casino: '…in the semblance of a small shipyard, it contains various rooms for different masters who work on different things, and there he keeps his alembics and every other artifice.'

One of the first fruits of the new Milanese presence must have been a circular plate of agate, described in 1577 by the Frenchman Audebert. In a space that was only as big as the palm of a hand, it presented a view of Florence 'so delicately that one could recognize the streets and squares as easily as in a large painting' (Audebert 1983).

The collaboration that Francesco sought from artists of differing origins and temperaments was not always a peaceful one. Contemporary documents, for example, record that the Gaffurri were great drinkers and card players, who easily came to blows with their fellow workers. However, this collaboration did prove extremely effective in terms of artistic results, as demonstrated by the famous lapis lazuli flask in the Museo degli Argenti (ill. 38) (*Magnificenza…* 1997). It was conceived in supremely elegant form by Buontalenti, carved by virtuoso masters from Milan, and exquisitely complemented by a gold and enamel mounting by the Flemish goldsmith Jacques Bijlivert (1550–1603). Francesco would also have liked to recruit the best specialists in the field of *commesso* work, but his 1568 attempt to obtain the passage from Rome to Florence of the highly sought-after 'Il Franciosino', or Giovanni Minardi, was thwarted and remained so. Since the small tables 'inlaid with jewels' that Vasari designed for Francesco (the existence of which was recorded by Vasari) have been lost, only a few other tables can be reasonably attributed to the age and tastes of the second Grand Duke (Giusti 1979; González Palacios 2001). These distinguish themselves from Roman examples as well as later Florentine ones in their emphasis on the fascinating beauty of the materials over the composition, which, in the well-known table from the Museo degli Argenti (ill. 40), displays an abstract geometry subordinated to the chilly splendour of the variegated jaspers that compose it (*Splendori…* 1988).

Having succeeded his brother in 1587, Francesco I completed the active transfer of the artistic workshops from the 'private delight' of the Casino di San Marco to the more office-like complex of the Uffizi in Florence itself. Following a coherent programme, which inextricably linked art and public life in a quintessentially Florentine and Medicean way, Vasari's building came to unite the State government with the artistic production and exhibition (in the Tribuna) of the flower of Grand Ducal collecting. Among the workshops already established by his brother and dedicated to the various types of furnishing, Ferdinando wanted to strengthen the *pietra dura* department in order to undertake the ambitious plans for the dynastic mausoleum in the

42

44. *The Rain of Manna*, completed in 1620 for the altar of the Cappella dei Principi and reused at the end of the eighteenth century. Florence, high altar of the Basilica di San Lorenzo

45. Tabletop with *View of the Port of Livorno*, completed by the Grand Ducal workshops in 1604, to the design of Jacopo Ligozzi. Florence, Uffizi

Cappella dei Principi (ill. 42) (Pampaloni Martelli 1979; Cresti in *Splendori...* 1988). Its construction began in earnest in 1604 but, as early as 1589, the Grand Ducal manufacture had been at work on panels for the internal revetment, which was to be completely in hardstones and polychrome marbles (ill. 43) and an unprecedented challenge for a building of such size (Przyborowski 1982). In the meantime, in 1590, the tireless Grand Duke, admiring the newly finished Niccolini Chapel in Santa Croce – the greatest example of polychrome architecture in Florence at that time – planned a chapel clad 'entirely with black marble from Vicenza, with panels of other veined marbles within, and with a mosaic vault', and another, similar one for the sanctuary at Loreto (Butters 2000).

But in the last decade of the century Francesco's finances and plans for an architecture in precious stones concentrated on a project to which he dedicated himself with the sovereign security that emanated from his motto, '*Maiestate tantum*'. The project must have seemed disproportionate even to an age accustomed to magnificence, for rumours soon circulated of the Grand Duke's secret plan to transport the Holy Sepulchre from Jerusalem to the Cappella dei Principi. In truth, and more modestly or perhaps more arrogantly, the great architectural adventure that would last over two centuries was intended only to exalt the Medici dynasty, entrusting only to the unchanging lustre of hardstones the proud affirmation of eternity in the sacred place of death.

The unconditional admiration with which the Cappella was greeted over its long but spectacular construction (A. González Palacios in *Splendori...* 1988) was matched from the outset by a lively attention to the novelty and rarity of its wall inlays, which can be traced back also to Rome. Equal industry was lavished on the 'jewel' that was to have been mounted in such a precious casket: the altar (ill. 44) surmounted by a Eucharistic tabernacle, a sparkling micro-architecture of hardstones and noble metals, exalted by and reflected in a cupola of rock crystal. The manufacture had almost completed this unprecedented marvel by the mid-seventeenth century but unfortunately it never reached its destination and was eventually dismantled and partially dispersed in the second half of the eighteenth century.

The parts that survive evoke its prodigious beauty. The echo it sounded throughout Florence even at the outset, when it was known through preliminary plans, is found in the extravagant apparatus of inlaid marbles on the high altar of Santo Spirito, created by the Michelozzi family between 1599 and 1607 (Giusti 1989; Acidini Luchinat 1996). The Grand Duke even generously 'lent' the artisans who executed its dazzling polychrome decorations. Another inlaid altar (ill. 43) from the same period (Giusti 1989 and 1997) is in the church of the Ognissanti, under the patronage of the illustrious Bardi family, who commissioned its design from the painter Jacopo Ligozzi (1547–1626), another artist from the inner Medici circle. Ligozzi's pictorial taste was probably responsible for privileging the fantasy and elegance of the stones over architectural design on the Ognissanti High Altar, especially in the *paliotto* with its three *Scenes from the Life of St Francis* inlaid and

46. Tabletop ornamented with flowers and panoplies, probably Roman from the end of the sixteenth century. Florence, Villa del Poggio Reale

47. Tabletop with parrot, vases of flowers and panoplies. Grand Ducal workshops, beginning of the seventeenth century. Hillerød, Castle of Frederiksborg, Nationalhistoriske Museum

48. Detail

49 and 50. Detail and overall view of a tabletop with parrot, vases of flowers and panoplies, executed in the Grand Ducal workshops between the end of the sixteenth century and the beginning of the seventeenth century. Florence, Museo dell'Opificio delle Pietre Dure

painted on *pietra paesina*, and in the altar cloth that seems to transmute by rare magic from embroidered linen into white marble quilted with coloured stones and mother of pearl.

It would be a mistake, however, to conclude that the creations of the recently founded Grand Ducal workshops focused exclusively on the demanding Cappella dei Principi: if anything, only some limit may have been placed on the production of hardstone vases (ill. 8). While maintaining the production so happily inaugurated by Francesco, Ferdinando I de' Medici also renewed his demands on the Saracchi and Fontana workshops, probably in order to allow the Milanese craftsmen who had transferred to Florence to concentrate on a genre of carving unknown to them – namely sculpture and mosaic in hardstones – and to perfect their mastery of the *commesso* technique.

Although they both entail working with hardstones, carving and inlay involve different working procedures, which are normally practised by different specialists. Thus, for example, in the court at Prague even the excellent Miseroni brothers were never called upon to execute the inlays so beloved by the Emperor Rudolf II. Moreover, during the seventeenth century a distinction in name and substance was also drawn in the Florentine Grand Ducal manufacture between the 'masters of inlay' and 'masters in relief'. Nonetheless, under Ferdinando I, Caroni and Gaffurri, who had been trained as vase-carvers, also tried their hands at the new figurative repertoire that the Grand Duke wished to introduce into *commesso* work, with immediately astounding results. Until then, this decorative genre had been almost exclusively abstract, whether the *peltae* and cartouches of the Roman tradition or the arcane geometries that intrigued Francesco de' Medici.

However, in this new endeavour Ferdinando did not suddenly abandon the antique marbles and classicist ornaments of the Roman inlays that he had known and appreciated at first hand during his long Roman sojourn as cardinal (ill. 46). It is enough to recall not only the many *alla romana* tables he commissioned, some probably made in Florence, but also the persistence of Roman materials and themes in a work that may even date back to the period of Cosimo II, the table for the Duke of Osuna, now in the Prado and finished in 1616 (González Palacios 2001).

But the revolution that Ferdinando encouraged and on which the vast and enduring fame of Florentine *commesso* work would depend was, in the Grand Duke's own words, a 'new way of representing in marbles inlaid together' a gamut of subjects practically as limitless as that in painting. In fact, it was with painting that stone mosaic now contended. The Mannerist inclination toward 'artifice' and the Counter-Reformation trend towards an illustrative and eloquent art merged together in this technique, which disting- uishes Florentine *commesso* from the ornamental inlays of the Roman school and transforms them into 'paintings in stone' intended to surprise and seduce (ill. 45). One of its first and most celebrated results of the new compositional repertoire in Grand Ducal inlays was the table, now lost, commissioned by the Emperor Rudolf II von Habsburg and executed by Stefano Caroni in 1589–97. Using Bohemian jaspers deliberately imported from the imperial territories, Caroni 'painted' a complex assortment of heraldic arms, panoplies, birds, landscapes and vases of flowers. The connoisseur Agostino del Riccio, a Florentine Domenican who was composing a *History of Stones* (Gnoli-Sironi 1996) in the same years, felt moved to underline the novelty that the table appeared 'all of one piece and not composed from marble or *bardiglio* [grey marble] or any other sort of marble, as they make tables in Florence and Rome.' In this way the limitations of traditional stone inlay were suppressed: the backing slab disappeared from view – the slab in which the inlays had been inset, checked and confined – and the polychrome composition could liberally expand like a puzzle composed with such precision that in the end it resembled a single image.

Although it might seem to be just an inlay of coloured marbles on a black background, a table in Frederiksborg (ill. 47) already corresponds to this new typology in its assembly of various stone sections. Alongside the predominantly Roman theme of military trophies, this table displays the naturalistic and essentially Florentine motifs of flowering vases and a parrot on a cherry branch that occupies the place of honour at the composition's heart. Very similar, though already more lively in both its overall design and individual elements, is another table in the Museo dell'Opificio delle Pietre Dure (Giusti 1979). Close to this in design is a third table in the Museum of the Synagogue in Rome (Giusti 1992), whose appearance goes to confirm the rapid degree to which the new taste for nature's spring-time subjects was establishing itself. Before too long its vivid palette, accentuated by a black background, would become the trademark of Florentine inlay.

Even so, intarsia did not disappear, either at that time or later, from Grand Ducal production. Moreover, until the end of Ferdinando I's reign, the initial predominance of nocturnal backgrounds in black, Belgian marble was always contested by a contrasting taste for symphonies of luminous and dazzling colours against a light background. A good example is a table in white marble at the Prado (ills. 57 & 204) (González Palacios 2001), recently 'brought back to life' in a restoration by the same Opificio that made it in the early 1600s. Here lapis lazuli, coral and coloured marbles fuse abstract ornaments of Mannerist stamp in their harmony of colour and design: from sophisticated vases naturalistically sprout the tulips which had been recently imported into Florence and become immediately fashionable; pairs of small birds still seem to preserve the traces of a flight only just concluded.

48

51

Yet *commesso* work appeared to be the most appropriate technique with which to attain an illusionistic and pictorial effect with the stones. At the beginning of the seventeenth century, in the Galleria dei Lavori, a series of masterpieces followed each other under Ferdinando's patronage, in incredibly swift succession when one considers their laborious complexity: the sparkling view of the port of Livorno (ill. 45) (*Splendori...* 1988) in the Uffizi table completed in 1604 by Cristofano Gaffurri (doc. 1575–1626) to the design of Jacopo Ligozzi; the iridescent slab of oriental chalcedony inlaid with vases, ears of grain, vine shoots and exotic birds (ill. 56) (*Magnificenza...* 1997) created by the Gaffurri workshop as an altar frontal for the Cappella dei Principi; the extraordinary and absolutely painterly series (ills. 44, 51 & 55) of sacred scenes and landscapes created in the first two decades of the seventeenth century for the altar of the Cappella to the cartoons of the major painters in the Medici circle and executed by its ever more numerous *commesso* masters (Giusti 1978 and 1979). Indeed, while the Caroni and Gaffurri undoubtedly launched hardstone inlays with their tried and tested expertise in carving, receptive and cultivated Florentines were soon capable of emulating their virtuosity. Both local craftsmen and 'German' masters would distinguish themselves in the enterprise; in the former category men like Francesco Ferrucci (1489–1530), of a family of porphyry specialists from Fiesole and the author of several inlay portraits (ill. 52) and floral decorations at the end of the sixteenth century. On the other hand Iacopo (Jakob) di Ian Flach stands out head and shoulders above the so-called 'German' masters present in the cosmopolitan Medici circle.

Florentine *commesso* work achieved a notable refinement in the well-established techniques of inlay, and the *opus sectile* of the Roman era. Although the latter had presented figurative subjects (ill. 53), and in calcareous marbles that were

easier to work, it had used rather large stone pieces that were better suited to striking effects of formal abstraction than the fluid pictorialism that was generally reserved for small tesserae mosaics in the Roman world. This pictorialism was instead the goal of the Grand Ducal inlays, and it was achieved by precision-cutting minute pieces of stone with profiles so articulate that they allowed the design to flow without rigidity. To this end it was necessary to cut the individual elements manually with extreme precision. Craftsmen used a small saw aided by an abrasive, achieving a millimetrical precision in defining the borders of the sections. After subsequent smoothing and polishing, the numerous joins were practically invisible in the final assembled piece (*Splendori...* 1988; Giusti 1992).

Besides these difficult 'mechanical' aspects of working, the range of stones chosen had a decisive bearing on the work's successful outcome, and needed to reconcile fidelity to

51. *Tuscan Landscape*, panel executed in the Grand Ducal workshops in 1605-8, to the design of the painter Bernardino Poccetti, for the altar of the Cappella dei Principi. Florence, Museo dell'Opificio delle Pietre Dure

52. *Portrait of Pope Clement VIII* in hardstone and marble inlay, given by Ferdinando I de' Medici to the Pope in 1601. Los Angeles, J. P. Getty Museum

53. *Head of the Sun God*, fragment of *opus sectile*, Roman artists of the third century AD. Rome, Museo Nazionale Romano

54. *Christ and the Samaritan*, detail of an aedicule in rock crystal, hardstones, gold and enamels, executed by the Grand Ducal workshops between 1591 and 1600. Vienna, Kunsthistorisches Museum

55. *The Last Supper*, finished by the Grand Ducal workshops in 1605, to the design of the painter Lodovico Cigoli, and then inserted into the eighteenth-century altar of the Cappella Palatina. Florence, Palazzo Pitti

the pictorial model with making best use of the colour palette of the stones themselves.

This in turn made it necessary to have a rich and variegated selection of stones, like those collected especially by the early Medici, on which to practise this patient and inspired research. The local historian Filippo Baldinucci (c. 1624–96), writing at the end of the seventeenth century, describes the process at length in these words: 'The best inlay-artist must...in every tiny and tiniest work of his, seek and find that little which nature has made on her own, which he intends to use for each of the infinite things that he wishes to represent that are of almost infinite colours; which task he can certainly not achieve without observing the infinite blots that are exhibited by the hardest gems and other stones, and thus primarily so he may become expert in painterly colouring' (Baldinucci 1975). In response to this need, on more than one occasion, and certainly in the cases of Lodovico Cigoli (1559–1613) (ill. 55) and Giovanni Bilivert (1576–1644), the painters who collaborated at the Galleria dei Lavori were entrusted with the task of 'finding the markings in hardstones'. Indeed, by the end of the eighteenth century the artist appointed to paint the models for manufacture, who had come for some time from the Habsburg-Lorraine family, also occupied the post of 'stone selector' (*sceglitore delle pietre*).

Alongside the new 'style' of stone mosaic, as Ferdinando himself called it, the Grand Duke sought still other challenges in stone carving for his hardstone manufacture. Besides the vases and cameos now guaranteed by tradition, a new genre of hardstone mosaic sculpture now also appeared. The oldest and precociously exceptional example of this genre to survive is the rock crystal aedicule now in Vienna (Fock 1974; Distelberger 2002), produced by the Caroni and Gaffurri workshops between 1591 and 1600, against whose inlaid fairy-tale landscape stand two fully modelled figures of *Christ and the Samaritan at the Well* (ill. 54). Here, for the first time, the two techniques in which Florence would lead for centuries are associated and perfectly harmonized: hardstone inlay in one of its first attempts at the landscapes that would become common during the seventeenth century; and the 'mosaic' sculpture achieved by assembling the different parts of the figure from separately cut hardstones of differing colours.

The surviving works, and the even more numerous ones recorded in documents, show that the reign of Ferdinando I was truly the apogee of the Grand Ducal manufacture in hardstone carving, which immediately leapt to the highest levels of excellence and became a forge of invention and production, capable of tackling the gargantuan enterprise of the altar and cladding of the Cappella dei Principi, as well as an unequalled series of courtly furnishings (Giusti 1997 and 2002).

The manufacturing fervour that Ferdinando imposed on the workshops also continued through the reign of his son Cosimo II, who prioritized works on the jewel-like altar of the

56. Detail of a tabletop of eighteenth-century assembly, formed from two panels made at the beginning of the seventeenth century and originally intended for the altar of the Cappella dei Principi. Florence, Galleria Palatina

57. Detail of a tabletop with an analogous subject, executed by the Grand Ducal workshops in the same period: vases of flowers and birds were among the naturalistic themes preferred for the Florentine inlays of the era of Ferdinando I de' Medici. An overall view of the table can be seen on p. 249. Madrid, Museo del Prado

58. *River Landscape*, executed in the first years of the seventeenth century in the Grand Ducal workshops for the altar of the Cappella dei Principi. Florence, Museo dell'Opificio delle Pietre Dure

59. Detail of the central panel of a cabinet executed *c.* 1620, with a view of the Villa Medici della Petraia, to a design by Giovanni Bilivert. Florence, Palazzo Vecchio

60. Tabletop known as the 'table of strewn flowers', executed by the Grand Ducal workshops in 1614-21, to the design of Jacopo Ligozzi, with details (ills. 61 & 62) on pp. 80-81. Florence, Uffizi

Cappella dei Principi. The landscape theme that had already made its appearance there in the Tuscan scenes realized in inlay after paintings by Bernardino Poccetti (1548–1612) was now increasingly motivated by the personal tastes of the new Grand Duke. Cosimo brought to his court a cosmopolitan circle of painters specializing in views and landscapes, in large part from northern Europe, which enjoyed an established tradition in these fields. It is therefore no coincidence that a certain Emanuele 'the German' designed some biblical scenes and two 'small landscapes' (ill. 58) planned for the altar. In scenes like *Samson Victorious over the Lion* and *Jonah and the Whale* this Emanuele made the landscape predominant, and in the coastal view with Jonah finally washed up on land the setting almost marginalizes the figure of the prophet among the craggy rocks and restless foaming of the sea. The same artist was probably responsible for two other landscapes in the Museo dell'Opificio, in which the rendering of the river scene and the buildings with stepped façades and pitched roofs is characteristically Nordic (Giusti 1978; *Splendori...* 1988). Another 'German' artist associated with hardstone inlay, and simply referred to as 'Fabiano', may be connected with the workshops established in Prague at the end of the sixteenth century on the initiative of Rudolf II von Habsburg and thanks to the 'importation' of Florentine inlay specialists.

It is no wonder that Cosimo II, who was interested in intensifying artistic ties between northern and southern Europe, would establish a tight rapport with Bohemian workshops. In this he was probably also encouraged by the presence of the eclectic Constantino de' Servi in the Galleria, an unusual artisan-cum-courtier who had previously sojourned for a long time at the court of Rudolf II von Habsburg. A connoisseur of the hardstone inlay of Prague, of which he possessed a few examples, the Grand Duke enlisted the Habsburg workshops in the fabrication of the altar for the Cappella dei Principi, and in 1610 sent them a design by Poccetti for *The Banquet of Abraham* (ill. 100). Translated into hardstone inlay in Prague in the workshop of the Florentine Castrucci, this panel was completed in around 1620 (*L'ombra del genio...* 2002).

The same decade saw the manufacture, this time in Florence, of a cabinet now in the Palazzo Vecchio, which distinguishes itself (and confirms Cosimo II's taste for such scenes) with a central panel on which a *View of the Villa della Petraia* (ill. 59) nestles among the customary vases of flowers, branches of fruit and birds. For this view, as a document of 1615 records, Cosimo had commissioned Giovanni Bilivert to paint 'coloured watercolours' as cartoons for inlays of the Medici villas visited by the artist during a riding tour, evidently in order to capture 'in the flesh' the luminous and changing light effects of a spring day like those represented in the Villa Petraia panel (Giusti 1979).

The urban scene at the centre of a cabinet that was formerly in the Residenz in Munich, which may well be of a similar date to the Villa Petraia cabinet, instead stands somewhere between fantasy and reality, with its telescopic view of the façade of Santo Spirito in Florence between two wings of classicized buildings.

By that time, only Jacopo Ligozzi remained from the old generation of painters once active for the first Grand Dukes. In this last decade of his service to the manufacture, he succeeded in making the principal and almost exclusive theme of hardstone inlays those compositions of birds, flowers and fruit with which he had always best demonstrated his analytical and captivating skill as a draughtsman of nature (Giusti 1978 and 1979; Conigello 1990; González Palacios 1993). This skill was well known to Francesco I de' Medici, for whom Ligozzi had executed a series of watercolour drawings of botanical and zoological subjects, now in the Uffizi (Bacci-Forlani Tempesti 1961). In these drawings the accuracy of representation, which anticipates scientific catalogues of the

63 and 64. Two examples of the 'caskets' produced in quantity by the Grand Ducal workshops in the Medici period: the first, of simple structure and with both figurative and abstract inlays, can be dated to the beginning of the seventeenth century. Munich, Bayerisches Nationalmuseum. The other is fully baroque in taste, and distinguished by its beautiful naturalistic panels and the fantastic gilded bronzes in which one may recognize the inventive design of Giovanni Battista Foggini. Paris, private collection

65. The famous *ex-voto* of Cosimo II de' Medici, in hardstones, enamels and diamonds, 1617–24. Florence, Museo degli Argenti

seventeenth century, attained aesthetic results that seem to distil the best of Cinquecento pictorial expertise. Thanks to Ligozzi, the phantasmagorical 'natural' world of stones that had risen out of the bowels of the earth, now opened up to embrace and interpret the other highly coloured expressions of nature that stud the earth like flowers, or plough the sky like birds.

It was also during the epoch of Cosimo II that the unsurpassed masterpieces in this genre were produced, like the *Table of strewn flowers* (ill. 60) now in the Uffizi (Giusti 1979; González Palacios 1993), a pulsing web of vegetation and animals eternalized in the intangible and enduring splendour of hardstones. What other palette in nature could compete with the azure shading of the bindweeds, the vibrant glimmer of the lilies of the valley and the dewy green of the foliage, or furnish the coloured iridescence of parrot feathers? This is what we are invited to conclude by the many tables (González Palacios 1993) in which this exotic bird rests – as though it had just escaped from the aviaries of the Boboli Gardens – on a nocturnal background of Flemish touchstone that heightens the chromatic harmonies of this 'living' nature, petrified by some beneficent spell.

And when life began to leave him, Cosimo II also entrusted his final memory to the fascinating and unalterable eloquence of the stones, portraying himself with all the regalia of Grand Ducal magnificence against the background of his native Florence. It is thus that he is portrayed on the very famous *ex-voto* (ill. 65) intended for the altar of St Charles Borromeo in Milan. However, this blaze of precious materials, which perhaps deliberately recalled sculptural jewels like the *St George and the Dragon* realized between 1586 and 1597 in Augsburg for the Duke of Bavaria, remained in Florence thanks to the premature death of the Grand Duke, and was only finished in 1624 by a team of four specialists who had dedicated seven years to the task. Two of them were artisans in hardstones, working on the mosaic relief of the figure of Cosimo II and the inlay view in the background; the goldsmith Cosimo Merlini worked on the altar frontal in embossed and chased gold which contained the relief, and which was cast in the eighteenth century; the jeweller Jonas Falck was responsible for the gems that incrusted the clothes, the crown and the sceptre (*L'ombra del genio...* 2002).

Another work started in the last years of Cosimo II and completed after his death in 1621 was the kneeler in the form of a small altar (ill. 69), formerly in the Villa at Poggio Imperiale (Giusti 1979). Made of ebony and hardstones, it displays a tessera mosaic of the *Baptism of Christ* in the frontispiece, where – according to a 1624 inventory – there once was a half-length *Magdalene*, now lost, by Leonardo da Vinci (1452–1519). Hardstones seemed to the Medici tastes of the time a worthy complement to a masterpiece by this most famous artist, included in a piece of furniture intended for Cosimo II's wife, Maria Maddalena of Austria (1587–1633), whose initials figure in the silver cartouches of the Ligozzi-like, hardstone frame surrounding the small panel. It is probable that the entire object, whose nobly severe taste corresponds well to that of the Grand Ducal widows Christine of Lorraine and Maria Maddalena of Austria, regents for their nephew and young son, was finished between 1621 and 1624, since the roses that are emblems of the new Grand Duke Ferdinando II, and his motto '*Gratia obvia vitio quesita*', already appear on the crowning piece.

Only in 1628 did Cosimo II's son, Ferdinando II, reach the age to rule. He then stayed at the helm of state for decades, until 1670. Under Ferdinando II, artistic life in general and the activity of the manufacture in particular resumed a busy rhythm, even if works on the altar for the Cappella dei Principi, which had been dear to his grandfather and father, first slowed and were then abandoned towards the middle of the century (Giusti 1997). Ferdinando preferred producing furnishings of regal pomp, which he frequently sent as gifts 'to the other great potentates of Europe' (as Baldinucci records)

66. Tabletop with flowers and fruits, Grand Ducal workshops, first quarter of the seventeenth century. Copenhagen, Rosenborg Castle

67. Detail

68. Tabletop with birds and landscape, Grand Ducal workshops, about the middle of the seventeenth century. Florence, private collection (unpublished)

and whose decorations were dominated by that naturalism inaugurated by Ligozzi (ill. 72).

An old and unexecuted project, the fruit of an artistic collaboration between the painters Ligozzi and Poccetti begun in the reign of Ferdinando I, was taken up and re-elaborated for the most representative work to issue from the manufacture during the reign of Ferdinando II: the great octagonal table (ill. 72) that celebrated his marriage with Vittoria della Rovere (Giusti 1979) and which was intended to stand in the Uffizi Tribuna, the temple of Medici treasures. It is no wonder that over sixteen years of work, from 1633 to 1649, and twelve craftsmen were needed to create this dizzying proliferation of shoots and branches, flowering vases, cornucopias, pearl-bearing shells, dolphins, as well as the heraldic arms of the spouses – all of which expand over a black background, sucking us into a decorative vortex in which we almost lose and abandon ourselves to the marvels of invention and the splendour of the materials.

Among the artists who worked on the definitive version of the Tribuna table was Baccio del Bianco (1604–57), an eclectic and cosmopolitan artist at the court of Ferdinando II who both designed furnishings and cultivated a personal inclination towards playful themes and caricature. The courtly creation for the Tribuna could certainly not entertain this particular tendency, but other inlays, mostly individual panels intended to be mounted on cabinets or tabletops (González Palacios 1993), did lend themselves to 'pleasing views...and portraits of persons with exaggerated expression' (ill. 80). So

69. Detail of the hardstone ornaments on a Medici kneeler in ebony, from 1621–24. Florence, Museo degli Argenti

70. Tabletop with the arms of the Elector of Bavaria, Grand Ducal workshops, c. 1623. Munich, Residenz

says Baldinucci, always well informed about the orientation and artistic novelties of seventeenth-century Florence.

The other magnificent furnishing that graced the Tribuna under Ferdinando II is less inspired by emergent and contemporary baroque tastes than by the prototypes of late Mannerism, a style that Florence continued to cultivate well into the seventeenth century. This is the solemn cabinet designed by Matteo Nigetti (c. 1560–1648), architect of the Medici mausoleum from the beginning of its construction (Giusti 1979). The cabinet is, in fact, a miniature building which follows a typology that would have suited the age of Ferdinando I as much as its hardstone inlays: the Ligozzian central panel, with its open terrace onto a lake view, and the exquisite grotesques and abstract decorations of the upper register with their vivid spring-time colours on a bright background of chalcedony. If there is anything new, it is the greater emphasis given to the sculptural ornaments in gilded bronze, which seem to point to the triumphal plasticity that would characterize the furnishings produced by the manufacture under the last Medici rulers.

It is fairly significant that, besides these superb examples, not much remains in Florence of hardstone production from the reign of Ferdinando II (ills. 65, 72 & 77), even though the manufacture thrived under him. Perhaps this is because many works were conceived from the outset as gifts to be sent elsewhere, in order to demonstrate Medici magnificence to their illustrious recipients. This must have been the case for the flowery tabletop that once belonged to Cardinal Antonio Barberini (1607–71), which was completed in 1658 (González Palacios 1993). Here the vegetal and zoological themes of the Ligozzian repertoire were amplified with baroque luxuriance to include a necklace of pearls in chalcedony at its centre, an illusionistic and evocative *trompe-l'oeil* destined for enduring success in the manufacture production until well into the eighteenth century (ill. 76 & 85).

To repay the gift of a portrait of Oliver Cromwell (1599–1658) sent by the statesman himself, the Grand Duke dispatched to England a *balsamario* (ill. 74) with panels in Florentine hardstone mosaic, still preserved in the Cromwell Museum at Huntingdon. These caskets of precious wood and hardstones were normally complemented by mountings in gilt bronze (ills. 63 & 64) and designed to contain precious trinkets or, in the case of the English box, perfumes and other refinements for the personal toilette. Who knows whether the austere puritan Cromwell would have appreciated them! They were sophisticated objects but less time-consuming

71. Tabletop from the beginning of the eighteenth century, representative of the late-baroque evolution of the traditional naturalistic themes in Grand Ducal inlays. Paris, private collection

72. Detail of the famous *Tavolo della Tribuna*, designed for the marriage of Ferdinando II de' Medici and in preparation between 1633 and 1644. Florence, Uffizi

73. Tabletop with flowers, fruits and cardinal birds, Grand Ducal workshops, second half of the seventeenth century. Vienna, Schloss Schönbrunn

MEDICEAN PRODUCTION IN FLORENCE

74. A 'balsamario', gift from Ferdinando II de' Medici to Oliver Cromwell. Huntingdon, Cromwell Museum

75. Detail of the hardstone inlays in a kneeler, Grand Ducal workshops, 1687. Florence, Palazzo Pitti

76. Tabletop with naturalistic ornaments and necklace of pearls, Grand Ducal workshops, mid-eighteenth century. Vienna, Kunsthistorisches Museum

than the tabletops that took years to produce, and they became a type of 'souvenir' that was frequently to leave the Florentine manufacture for the most far-flung destinations.

In the lively circle of exchange that particularly involved the applied arts in Medici Florence of the second half of the seventeenth century, making the capital of the small Grand Duchy anything but a peripheral centre, the Grand Duke summoned the most talented international artisans to work at his workshop, in many cases permanently.

Thus, the Flemish Leonard van der Vinne arrived in Florence by 1659 and was active in the Galleria as 'first ebonist and inlay artist' until his death in 1713 (González Palacios 1986). Van der Vinne was responsible for the precocious introduction into Florence of a decorative style developed in the Low Countries just after the middle of the century, and divulgated from there to the France of the Sun King, Louis XIV. This style featured wooden inlays of sumptuous floral design, which were combined with precious and variegated materials, as well as ivory and mother-of-pearl in seductive colour schemes. 'Il Tarsia', as this Flemish master came to be known in Florence, executed exclusively wooden furniture, but often collaborated on furniture that included the customary hardstone mosaics, often also floral and therefore both technically and thematically complementary to the inlays by Leonard van der Vinne.

In 1670 the long reign of Cosimo II was followed by that of Cosimo III (b. 1642), who would rule Tuscany for over half a century until his own death in 1723. Shortly thereafter the Medici dynasty would die out, but the political and administrative decline of the Grand Duchy was already manifest in the reign of Cosimo III, flying in the face of his proud *impresa* and its motto '*Certa fulgent sidera*'.

Stars gave way to a golden twilight, at least in terms of the enduring brilliance of the court manufacture, whose creations were supreme among the applied arts of European baroque. Even more than his father, who had already culti-

75

vated the cosmopolitan nature of the Grand Ducal manufacture and the international diffusion of their creations, Cosimo III poured his passion and wealth into the enterprise that his great-grandfather Ferdinando I had initiated almost a century earlier.

The working of other precious materials now stepped up alongside long-favoured hardstones (ills. 71 & 75): ivory was worked by specialists from German-speaking countries, including the Bavarian Philip Senger or Balthasar Permoser, one of the major sculptors of baroque Europe; tortoiseshell and amber were entrusted to the tried and tested expertise of other Nordic masters; the always excellent van der Vinne was joined by the Frenchman Riccardo Bruni in working ebony and inlays in different woods.

Cosimo III also ensured that the young sculptors were educated and kept up to date on the baroque at its source, Rome, by establishing a Grand Ducal Academy there. The Rome experience did not fail to cause a flowering of invention in the Galleria dei Lavori, which also saw the activity of Massimiliano Soldani Benzi, Carlo Marcellini and Giovanni Battista Foggini (1652–1725). From 1694 until his death, Foggini would be the artistic superintendent of the harmonious activity of the manufacture.

The baroque predilection for the plastic, and the emerging role of sculptors in the Medici Galleria, which had been dependent on painters for hardstone compositions in the past, ensured that under Cosimo III sculptural treatment of hardstones (ill. 78) found venues and specializations never previously attempted. Among the full-time artisans in the manufacture 'panel masters' (*maestri in piano*) worked alongside 'carving masters' (*maestri in rilievo*) and these categories were subdivided into further specializations, like the *fruttisti* or inlay artists who carved those in-the-round hardstone fruits that sprout from vegetal festoons in gilt bronze and which are among the happiest inventions of the period. This invention would reappear in numerous sacred and secular

furnishings, in different forms and arrangements but always with an extraordinary decorative impact: whether the minuscule and reflective bunches of amethysts, jaspers, quartzes and cornelians that garland the triumphal series of reliquaries commissioned by the extremely pious but far from humble Grand Duke for the palace chapel (Bertani-Nardinocchi 1995); or the fleshy fruits that seduce and trick sight and touch, sprouting from vibrant bronze foliage that envelops a painting by Carlo Dolci (ill. 79), which was Cosimo III's wedding gift to his son Gian Gastone (1671–1737) in 1697 (Giusti 1979).

Among the various and able carving masters emerged the superlative expertise of Giuseppe Antonio Torricelli (1659–1719) (ill. 83), 'sculptor of hardstones and cameos' as contemporary records define him, capable of modelling the hardest stones in both relief and three dimensions with a softness and subtlety of transition that makes them look like wax. It is noteworthy that the young Torricelli's earliest apprenticeship was to the famous wax-modeller Gaetano Zumbo. One can only conclude that Torricelli's most able hands magnificently reproduced the ductile docility of the wax when he applied himself to working on a material of a completely different consistency.

One almost fears melting, with the warmth from one's hand, the tender Christ Child on the *Reliquary of the Crib* (ill. 81) (*Splendori...* 1988), below whose palpitating and infantile nudity the chalcedony sheet dips and rises in fluffy eddies just like a cloud.

Both this and other creations by Torricelli derive from models by Foggini, who was brilliant in both his conception of plastic form and decorative invention, capable of marrying the Roman baroque scenography he had witnessed during a youthful sojourn with the graphic subtlety and material hedonism of Florentine tradition. The most outstanding masterpiece to demonstrate this marriage is the kneeler for the Grand Duke's favourite daughter Anna Maria Luisa, the

77. Table cabinet with panels in Florentine inlay, from about the middle of the seventeenth century. Schwerin, Staatliches Museum

wife of the Palatine Elector, sent to Düsseldorf as a gift in 1706, a piece of furniture-cum-sculpture in which the dark luminosity of ebony blossoms through the hardstones carved by Torricelli and the bronzes modelled by Foggini (*Splendori...* 1988).

Another spectacular piece of furniture sent by the Grand Duke to the court of the Elector was the cabinet of the Elector Johann Wilhelm, husband of Anna Maria Luisa, finished in 1709 and conceived as a monument of dynastic celebration (ill. 84) (*Splendori...* 1988). It is almost a temple whose central niche is dedicated to the display of the Prince, 'heroically' armed but seated on military trophies to symbolize that vigilant peace to which the crowning bronze allegories of Magnanimity and Fortitude also attest. The sculptural flair of Foggini, who designed the cabinet, plastically and dynamically transformed the calmly architectural models for cabinets produced by the Galleria in the seventeenth century: a unique and brilliant decorative solution links the wooden basement animated by cartouches and bronze volutes; the central corps still maintains the Florentine regularity of harmonious architectural articulation, despite the ornate profusion of reliefs and hardstone inlays; the crown is a theatrical crescendo of sculptural form.

In this case too the quality of Foggini's invention is combined with the skill of the craftsmen, including Torricelli, to produce what may be counted among the greatest master-

78. Ebony casket, with sculptures and appliqués in gilt bronze, hardstone inlays and reliefs, Grand Ducal workshops, before 1694. Munich, Bayerisches Nationalmuseum

79. Detail of the elaborate frame around a painting by Carlo Dolci, in ebony, hardstones and gilded bronze, a gift from Cosimo III de' Medici for the marriage of his son Gian Gastone, in 1697. Florence, Palazzo Pitti

80. Nineteenth-century table with caricature scenes representative of one trend of seventeenth-century production at the Grand Ducal workshops, inspired by the drawings of Baccio del Bianco. New York, private collection

81. *Reliquary of the Crib* in rock crystal, hardstones and gilt silver. *The Christ Child* in chalcedony is the work of Giuseppe Antonio Torricelli, 1697. Florence, Museo degli Argenti

82. *Adoration of the Magi*, polychrome relief in hardstone inlay, carved in 1705 by Torricelli for the door of the tabernacle in the Cappella Palatina. Florence, Palazzo Pitti

83. *Bust of Vittoria della Rovere*, hardstone sculpture by Torricelli, *c.* 1697. Florence, Museo degli Argenti

pieces in the field of decorative arts. But even the 'minor' production of jewel boxes, table clocks, frames, wall paintings and many items of furniture display an unerring quality in which luxury and refinement combine in a rare equilibrium. The same equilibrium runs through the numerous but never repetitive variations on the theme of the fresco of the *Annunciation*, which was venerated and famous throughout Florence and had already appeared in hardstone works under Ferdinando I. But it was Cosimo III in particular who esteemed this work a precious *souvenir*, doubly appropriate as a testimony to Florentine art and devotion. The *Annunciation* figures appear once more in a vibrant water-stoup, another gift to the Palatine Electress in 1704, in which the minuscule chalcedony shell that serves as the drip pan almost disappears in the riot of gilt bronze angels, *ramages*, festoons and rays made by Foggini, and which frame two hardstone ovals of the *Angel* and the *Virgin Annunciate*.

But Foggini's sculptural imagination did not fail to yield its best fruits on those exceptional occasions in which he lent designed cartoons for flat inlays. More often than not these had been previously entrusted to the painters who collaborated with the manufacture, among them the *fiorante* (flower specialist) Andrea Scacciati. Among the last products of Foggini's direction of the Grand Ducal manufacture is the rightly famous table of 1716 in the Galleria Palatina (ill. 85) (*Splendori...* 1988), in which the central 'tray' of botanical motifs of old Ligozzian stamp is shaped with a graphic verve that anticipates the rococo, while iridescent and heraldic plumed dolphins spring from the corners to resurrect the bizarre metamorphoses of Mannerist invention. This superlative 'anthology' of the manufacture repertoire (ill. 85), now almost at the end of its Medicean golden age, fortunately preserves its original base – a rarity as most bases have disappeared from other hardstone tables because of the successive substitutions of changing taste. The slab of Flemish touchstone is still encased in a frame of chased and gilded bronze, enriched with corner scrolls, and rests on ebony pilasters clad with hardstones and draped in bronze festoons.

Scintillating naturalistic fantasies on a touchstone background also animate the tables sent to the Elector of Bavaria (ill. 86) and the King of Denmark (González Palacios 1986) by the always munificent Cosimo III, who with the fading of the Medici star seems to have wished to mark its luminous trail across the European skies. At his behest or at least with his consent, works and artisans emigrated to testify to the merits of Florentine manufacture abroad. For example, the carving specialist Francesco Mugnai moved to Kassel at the end of the seventeenth century after the Landgrave Karl of Hesse-Kassel, in a visit to Florence, managed to obtain permission from the Grand Duke for Mugnai to transfer him to his court 'to serve in the same profession'.

The prolific Torricelli continued to excel in the Grand Ducal manufacture, creating an 'imperial' cameo of Cosimo III, in which portrayer and portrayed apparently wish to compare themselves with the great cameos of imperial Roman tradition. Yet, despite the technical excellence of the manufacture they did not close themselves up in glorious isolation, for in 1714 Cosimo III felt it necessary to send Torricelli in person to Milan to 'update' and inform himself on the techniques used there for hardstone carving. Milan had already established itself in the field in the Renaissance and had evidently maintained its level of quality. Torricelli, whose long activity was near conclusion on his death in 1719, brought back a detailed report entitled *Drawings of the tools for working Hardstones used in Milan, for the use of the Most Serene Grand Duke of Tuscany*, which seems partially to have inspired the old working benches still preserved in the Museo dell'Opificio (Giusti 1992b).

During the rather brief reign of the last Great Duke, Gian Gastone (r. 1723-37), as much a lover of the arts as his predecessors but now entering the 'twilight' of the family's imminent demise, it is symbolic that the only truly large-scale creation of the Grand Ducal manufacture only saw the light thanks to the Duke of Beaufort, who commissioned it for a sum that was huge even for the times. This was the monumental cabinet executed between 1726 and 1732 that seems to be the last worthy epilogue to the *grand goût* of baroque furnishings initiated by the Medici manufacture (González Palacios 1990).

The international prestige that the manufacture had gained itself lessened its risk of dying along with the Medici dynasty that had created and reared it with such passion. But in the uncertainty following the death of Gian Gastone, in 1737, no fewer than ten masters from the manufacture accepted the invitation of Charles of Bourbon (1716–88) and transferred to Naples giving life to a new workshop, the third Florentine 'branch' after Prague and Paris. The diaspora was led by Francesco Ghinghi, Torricelli's former rival in carving, whose autobiography does not fail to pay nostalgic homage to the memory of the Medici 'true and legitimate patrons of all the virtues and the noble Arts' (González Palacios 1984).

An unbeatable age in Florentine hardstone carving was drawing to a close, but a new and still fecund period was beginning under the patronage of another great House, that of the Habsburg-Lorraines, who, thanks to an agreement between the international powers in 1737, succeeded the Medici family on the throne of the Grand Duchy of Tuscany.

84

84. The monumental *Cabinet of the Palatine Elector*, a gift from Cosimo III de' Medici to his son-in-law Johann Wilhelm in 1709. Florence, Museo degli Argenti

85. Tabletop with naturalistic ornaments and heraldic emblems, executed in the Grand Ducal workshops in 1716, to the design of Giovanni Battista Foggini. Florence, Galleria Palatina

86 and 87. Tabletop given by Cosimo III de' Medici to the Elector of Bavaria, first decades of the eighteenth century. Munich, Nymphenburg Castle

Chapter 4

The Fortunes of Hardstone Inlay in Seventeenth-Century Europe

If a passion for artistic wizardry in stone became diffuse throughout sixteenth-century Europe, it was largely thanks to the circulation of designs and artists that determined, during the course of the century, the international face of the Renaissance. The most magnificent period in the art of hardstone inlay, which took place outside Italy but was still solidly linked to it, began in Prague at the end of the 1500s in the exalted milieu of the court of Rudolf II von Habsburg. Emperor from 1576, Rudolf had established his capital in Bohemia and made Prague a fervent cultural and artistic centre of broad cosmopolitan horizons (*Prag um 1600*, 1988). Here rare stones resumed as important a place in the imperial trappings as they had under the rule of Charles IV of Bohemia (r. 1346–78), when Prague had been one of the capitals of international Gothic.

Although the Emperor was certainly not the only European sovereign or lord to indulge a passion for both sculpted hardstone vases and polychrome inlays, he did set the example for the courts of France, Naples and Spain by initiating the specialized manufacture of these artefacts in the service of his court. In this he took his cue from the workshop that his contemporary and 'associate' in artistic taste, Ferdinando I de' Medici, had established in Florence. Like Ferdinando, Rudolf set about stockpiling the raw materials, primarily by obtaining masses of variegated jaspers from the territories of Bohemia, which was so replete with them that in the seventeenth century it became proverbial that the stone the cow-herder threw at his cow was more valuable than the cow itself. Although Bohemian jaspers became the material of choice for inlay, especially in the *commessi* of Prague manufacture, other stones were imported into the imperial capital and to obtain them the Emperor dispatched emissaries to other territories rich in precious minerals, such as Baden and Alsace (Fischer 1971); and even further afield, seeking to obtain through his ambassador to the Spanish court exotically veined jaspers and agates from India.

The most beautiful stones collected were sent by Rudolf to Milan to be worked into cameos and vases in the workshops there that specialized in gem cutting, and whose supremacy was universally recognized by the premier collectors of Europe. The Medici of Florence had followed the same practice, until Francesco de' Medici took the initiative of inviting a workshop of Milanese artisans to his court in 1572, thereby appropriating to his city and exclusive service an activity that Milan had until then virtually monopolized. Whether in the spirit of emulation or from parallel motiva-

88. Detail of an altar with stone inlays, by the Corbarelli workshop, artisans of Florentine origin active throughout the seventeenth century in the centres of northern Italy. Padua, church of Santa Giustina

89. *Lady with a Fan*, cameo in polychrome stone inlay, executed by Ottavio Miseroni in Prague, *c.* 1610. Vienna, Kunsthistorisches Museum

90

91

90. *St Mary Magdalene*, cameo in polychrome stone inlay, executed by Ottavio Miseroni in Prague, c. 1610. Vienna, Kunsthistorisches Museum

91. *The Mulatto Woman*, agate cameo, Miseroni workshop in Milan, c. 1560. Vienna, Kunsthistorisches Museum

92. *Landscape with Bridge and Chapel*, hardstone inlay executed in Prague by the Florentine Cosimo Castrucci, 1596. Vienna, Kunsthistorisches Museum

tions, the Emperor now also proved unwilling to share the virtuosity of the Milanese engravers with other patrons and over such a distance: on 22 January 1588, Ottavio Miseroni (1567–1624), the son of Girolamo, entered Rudolf's service with a salary of fifteen florins a month; he was only young but already highly skilled and had headed one of the most celebrated workshops for gem-cutting (Kris 1929; Distelberger 1983 and 1999).

Ottavio Miseroni remained active in Prague until his death, working for the court and collaborating with goldsmiths and jewellers in the service of the Emperor, but still maintaining close ties with his father's workshop in Milan, which was run from 1600 by his stepbrother Giovanni Ambrogio (c. 1551/52–1616), and from whom Rudolf II also commissioned various works. Ottavio's activity in Prague was particularly intense and felicitous as long as Rudolf II lived and he therefore enlisted the help of his two brothers, Alessandro and Aurelio, bringing them over specially from Milan (*Distelberger* 2002). Eventually he left the family workshop to his son Dionisio, who was assumed into the service of the imperial court shortly before Ottavio's death.

In the vases he created for Rudolf II, Ottavio was able to adapt the refined gem-cutting technique he had learnt in Milan to the softly sensual sculptural style favoured by the artists of court. The most celebrated of these were Adriaen de Vries (1545–1626), who had been a pupil of Giambologna (1529–1608) in Florence, the ivory carver Nikolaus Pfaff (1556?–1612) and the goldsmith Paulus van Vianen (c. 1570–1613). In 1608 van Vianen executed the gold mounting for one of the first vases that Ottavio made for the Emperor, a ewer on which a dragon with bats' wings carved in amber-hued chalcedony is held prisoner by a golden siren that sinuously emerges from the waves of the cover. In such hardstone vases produced in Prague, just like those from the Grand Ducal workshops of Florence, the carved stone vies with the gold mounting to create an image of rarefied and fantastic beauty, reciprocally exalting the preciousness of the constituent materials. An excellent example is the celebrated product of a stimulating collaboration between Miseroni and the goldsmith Jan Vermeyen (before 1559–1608), a green jasper cup with blood-red markings, modelled in the form of a niche with vibrant palmettes in very low relief, and surmounted by a golden statuette of Bacchus, seated on a border with a gold and enamel fascia.

Besides the prevailing production of vases, Ottavio also set his skills to cameos, another type of glyptic product usually practised by carving experts, and not long after his arrival in Prague he executed a chalcedony cameo with the profile of Rudolf II, conserved in the Kunsthistorisches Museum (Distelberger 2002). But his detailed carving technique matured and culminated twenty years later in the *commesso* cameos of polychrome stones, which introduced to Prague a new genre of mosaic relief that had been pioneered in Florence under Ferdinando I de' Medici. The first Medicean attempts at this technique, like the *Christ and the Samaritan* (ill. 54) fully modelled from various coloured stones, were twenty years older than the *Lady with a Fan* (ill. 89) and the *Magdalene* (ill. 90) that Miseroni executed about 1610 as great oval cameos in which the figure is a relief of several coloured stones cut separately and then pieced together (Distelberger 2002).

From a technical point of view, this was a sculptural transposition of tabletop inlay (*commesso in piano*), the form of hardstone mosaic that had reached the pinnacle of virtuosity in complex decorative and figurative images in Florence at the end of the 1580s. The sophisticated taste that esteemed the technical and conceptual complexity of works that seemed painted but were instead made of stone, which appeared to be a single but in fact concealed an expert juxtaposition of discrete elements, found a parallel and attractive field for experiment in three-dimensional hardstone *commesso*. In Florence, the new invention of the Caroni and Gaffurri workshops was to concentrate on in-the-round figures, perhaps because they were more in line with the living sculptural tradition of Florentine Mannerism, but also because of their unheralded technical difficulties, which for the Medici manufacture were a goal and a challenge to overcome. In Prague, Ottavio Miseroni preferred to adapt the plastic *commesso* of the cameo, a genre that was part and parcel of his personal artistic and technical experience, and which had been one of the most sought-after products of the Milanese carving workshops from the early sixteenth century.

It is also probable that the idea of creating a polychrome cameo, executed with stones of varying colour, was instigated by the virtuoso subtlety of the Milanese cameo-cutters. These men were capable of selecting with surprising ability the markings of a single stone, exploiting the different areas of colour in such a way that they would match, for example, the brown of hair, the clarity of skin or the shifting colours of drapery. They created superb pieces that could withstand the perpetual comparison with the works of antiquity. Witness, for example, among the many 'polychrome' cameos that issued from the atelier of the Miseroni, *The Mulatto Woman* (ill. 91) realized towards 1560, in which one remains uncertain whether to admire more the refinement of the carving or the miraculous correspondence between the palette of the stone and the formulation of the image (Distelberger 2002).

Another highly refined creator of cameos of this kind was the Milanese Alessandro Masnago (c. 1560–1620), whom Rudolf II preferred to commission. In works such as the *Lucretia*, Masnago modulated with exquisite sensibility the red-white bichromy of the agate to render the flesh and robe of the heroine (Distelberger 2002). He was so successful that one might suppose that a cameo of this sort, already in the imperial collection in Prague by the end of the century, inspired the young Ottavio Miseroni in his still modest attempt at a cameo, the *Madonna* of around 1600, based on a similar chromatic distinction (Distelberger 2002). An altogether greater surety and refinement of carving is evident, a decade later, in Ottavio's polychrome reliefs, which contain vivid chromatic contrasts, impossible to obtain with natural veining, however fantastic, within a single stone. For example, the medallion of *St Mary Magdalene* (ill. 90), a real piece of bravura assembled from over fifty pieces and which Ottavio signed, displays some studied refinements of conception and execution such as the interweaving of the agate veil with the cornelian hair, or the folds of the undergown in white chalcedony that poke through the slits in the sleeves of red jasper.

In this new genre of cameo, in which the composition is enriched with details made possible by the differing patterns of the stones, Miseroni obtained unprecedented pictorial effects with a strong aesthetic impact. At the same time he circumvented the difficulties posed by 'monolithic' cameos, in which the artist necessarily combined fantasy and fatigue to temper his creative impetus to the capriciousness of the markings in the stone (Bukovinska 1988). This did not mean, however, that Miseroni and his Prague workshop abandoned traditional cameo carving, which continued to be practised, and indeed with greater frequency than the polychrome variety (Distelberger 2002). Indeed we have the evidence of two cameos from the last phase of Ottavio's career, one a *Virgin* and the other a *St Anne*, medallions that decorate the casings of two aedicule reliquaries of around 1620, entirely composed of jasper and enriched with gems, pearls and golden mountings (Distelberger 2002). Yet, despite the preciousness of their stones, this pair of reliquaries does not attain the harmonious elegance of the creations of the period of Rudolf II, and even the two *commesso* reliefs, which were probably produced by studio assistants, do not exhibit the compositional fluidity and subtleties of workmanship that we see in the cameos made ten years earlier.

Furthermore, Miseroni's activity after the death of Rudolf II, in 1612, experienced a progressive decline due to the waning interest in the arts of his successors to the imperial throne and because of turbulent political developments. The operational and economic difficulties in which the Miseroni workshop now found itself are also reflected in the evolution of its style, which became ever drier and more abstract, losing that fluid softness which had previously characterized it. Yet, with the passage of the workshop from father to son, Ottavio's heir Dionisio (c. 1607–61), vase-carving in hardstones experienced a new and happier season, thanks to the favour accorded him by the Emperor Ferdinand III (r. 1637–57) and the inventive and technical flair that he was able to demonstrate. Miseroni now occupied several important posts in the Prague court (Distelberger 2002). Abandoning the production of cameos and polychrome reliefs inaugurated by his father, Dionisio concentrated on vase-carving, particularly in quartz and rock crystal (Distelberger 2002). Numerous and varied examples were turned out by his workshop, which at mid-century numbered no fewer than fourteen craftsmen. However, the accession to the throne of the Emperor Leopold I (r. 1658–1705) marked the definitive decline of the Miseroni workshop, which passed after Dionisio's death, in 1661, to his son Ferdinand Eusebius. The latter principally devoted his labours to completing the vases left unfinished by his father and did not measure up to his father in his autograph works. On Ferdinand Eusebius's death, in 1684, the various unfinished pieces left in the studio were sent to the court in Vienna, to be evaluated and completed by the craftsmen who worked there. Thus concluded, after almost a century, the glyptic activity that Rudolf II had succeeded in founding in Prague.

The Prague workshop for marble *commesso*, also established by Rudolf II, had a shorter but more intense and illustrious history. Rudolf II's governing passion for hardstones found double nourishment in the sophisticated artistic creations obtained with these noble materials and in the physical and magical properties that he recognized in these singular creations of nature. One testimony to the scientific-alchemical culture in vogue at the court of Rudolf (one of its many parallels with the Medicean court of Francesco I) is the *Gemmarum et lapidarum historia*, published in 1609 by Anselmus Boetius de Boodt, the Emperor's personal physician. This work, half-way between the emerging science of the

93. *Landscape with Obelisk*, inlay panel in hardstones executed in Prague by Giovanni Castrucci in the first or second decade of the seventeenth century. Vienna, Kunsthistorisches Museum

94

classification of the natural world and the abiding faith in the supernatural properties of stones, contains a eulogy – not just courtly – to Rudolf II's erudition on stones.

As de Boodt says, Rudolf was motivated by the fact that 'in noble stones you may contemplate the greatness and unspeakable power of God, who unites in bodies so small the beauty of the entire world and the force of all other things, and in this way you have always before your eyes a certain reflection and spark of divinity.'

At the time de Boodt was writing, the Emperor's *Kunstkammer* counted among its hardstone treasures many examples of recent *commesso* work. Rudolf had taken an interest in this genre for years, beginning in 1585 when he charged his ambassador to Rome with finding an expert master 'to prepare and work tabletops and all those sorts of things that can be made', drawing on the reserves of jaspers and hardstones in the imperial stores (Neumann 1957). However, it was from Florence that the first taste of splendour arrived, from the newborn Medici manufacture, and next the artisans who would transplant Florentine mosaic to Prague. By 1589, a year after the foundation of the Galleria dei Lavori, Ferdinando I de' Medici sent as a gift to Rudolf II a table, now lost but which the Venetian ambassador to the court of Prague described as 'set with crystals and other stones, esteemed to be of singular creation and great value.' The table excited the enthusiasm of the Emperor so much that in the same year he commissioned a second table from the Medici manufacture, sending them Bohemian jaspers for the purpose and sustaining all the costs of its fabrication.

This mythical table, whose execution took eight years, has also been lost. But numerous contemporaries enthused over its exceptional quality, among them connoisseurs such as the Florentine del Riccio, who watched its progress, and de Boodt, who saw it arrive in Prague in 1597 accompanied by Ambrogio Caroni, whose workshop had produced it (Neumann 1957; Fock 1974, 1982, 1988). Thanks to their descriptions, we know that the centre of the tabletop featured the Emperor's monogram composed from slivers of garnet

94. *Holy Magdalene in Prayer*, Castrucci workshop, *c.* 1615–22. Vienna, Kunsthistorisches Museum

95. *Sacrifice of Isaac*, Castrucci workshop, *c.* 1610. Vienna, Kunsthistorisches Museum

95

mounted in gold, surrounded by landscapes, military trophies, birds and flowers connected with a vegetal frieze. These were all 'pictorial' subjects that Florentine mosaic had perfected, and thereby affirmed that Florence had moved beyond the abstract decorations of Roman *commesso* work from which she had taken her first cues.

Perhaps an echo of the lost table, which remained in the Habsburg collections for the entire seventeenth century, may be found in one executed in Prague by the Castrucci workshop for Charles I of Liechtenstein (1569–1627), between 1619 and 1623 (Vincent 1985; Distelberger 2002). Not coincidentally Charles I had been one of Rudolf II's most intimate collaborators as well as responsible for the artistic workshops. In this table, which is among the last superb works in *commesso* to leave the Prague workshops, the fluidity of the design and execution of the individual elements seems 'frozen' by a rigorous geometricized framework that looks back to a still Cinquecento and Italianized taste. Here too, as in Rudolf II's table, figure landscapes, military trophies, coats of arms and monograms, and the dividing bands of jasper are bordered by garnets mounted in gilt bronze fillets. This motif has been rightly considered characteristic of Prague workmanship, but we have seen that its first appearance was on the tabletop prepared for the Emperor in Florence, the success of which induced Rudolf to seek out in Florence the desired master who could give life to a *commesso* workshop in Prague.

This wish came true with the emigration to Prague of Cosimo Castrucci, from a family of Florentine jewellers, who had entered imperial service by 1592, when a safe-conduct for a journey from Prague to Italy defines him as 'inlayer of hardstones to His Majesty' (Distelberger 2002). And so Cosimo appears on the scene in his oldest work yet known, a hardstone inlay panel signed and dated 1596 (ill. 92). This panel shows him to have been a master of the 'pictorial' technique perfected by the Medici manufacture, and already perfectly in line with the artistic tastes of his illustrious patron, in his ability to stage an airy landscape view, the genre that had made its appearance in Florentine inlay only in the table for Rudolf II.

Castrucci is not recorded among the artisans active in the Florence manufacture, but at the time of the first Grand Dukes the *commesso* technique was not exclusive to the Medici workshops. It was also practised throughout Florence by 'independent' masters, like the Giuliano Balsimelli that del Riccio records as a great *commesso* specialist and who, in 1585, executed the inlaid altar of the Niccolini Chapel in Santa Croce (Giusti 1997). When Castrucci moved to Paris he must already have been in command of a tech-

96. *View of Prague*, Castrucci workshop, after 1606. Several versions of this subject were made by Castrucci, always inspired by contemporary prints. Vienna, Kunsthistorisches Museum

nique which even the able hardstone carver Ottavio Miseroni did not practise, in contrast to his Milanese 'colleagues' in Florence, the Caroni and Gaffurri, who added inlay work (so favoured by Ferdinando I de' Medici) to their original skills in the glyptic arts.

It is clear that Cosimo Castrucci did not enjoy the esteem of the connoisseur Costantino de' Servi (1554–1622), an eclectic Florentine gentleman involved in the Medici manufacture. In a letter sent to his homeland from Prague in 1604, de' Servi wrote 'as far as *commesso* work is concerned, there is no other than Castrucci...and he jealously watches me because he is fearful that I will say something to His Majesty.' But perhaps de' Servi felt a little jealous too. He had been well established in Prague and court circles since 1573 and now saw another Florentine enjoy the much sought-after imperial favour.

Moreover, the rare works that can be ascribed to Castrucci with some certainty demonstrate a refinement of technical execution and above all a sensitive evaluation of the chromatic qualities of the materials.

One of the difficulties in identifying the autograph works of Castrucci is the precocious presence in Prague of his son Giovanni, who is recorded there by 1598 and who in 1610 was nominated Carver of Precious Stones to the Imperial Treasury. Giovanni may have received this post after the death of his father, which is not recorded, but Cosimo could not have been active for long if one considers that an imperial inventory drawn up from 1606 to 1616 lists fourteen works in *commesso*, all of which are ascribed to Giovanni Castrucci. Giovanni must have been a prolific artist, anything but inferior to his father, as has been recently suggested (Distelberger

2002). Indeed I believe that this hypothesis is proven by securely attributed works (ill. 93); the frequency and prestige of his imperial commissions; and, finally, the fact that Giovanni was very esteemed in the extremely demanding environment of the Medici manufacture. He was so esteemed, in fact, that on two occasions, in 1602 and 1610, it was planned to include him among the masters of the Galleria dei Lavori (Przyborowski 1982; Fock 1982 and 1988).

Whatever the case, in the 1596 panel of his father, Cosimo, one may recognize an already complete expression of the style that will characterize Prague inlay for at least three decades. These characteristics focus on the evocation of nature (ill. 94), rendered in the dewy and vibrant tones of the jaspers of Bohemia and Alsace, with sharper and more vivid patterning used to represent architecture and foreground images, and other pieces dissolving into smoky and vibrant colours to express evanescent distance. With these 'romantic' landscapes, inspired by the Flemish and German painters favoured by the Emperor, and marked by a sense of the threatening and mysterious presence of nature, Prague inlays find their distinctive style. This style immediately gave them an originality absent from the Florentine mosaics of which they were nonetheless direct descendants, and with which they would maintain recurrent ties.

Nor is it improbable that the landscape vocation of the Prague inlays had influenced the affirmation of a landscape tendency in Florentine inlays of the first decade of the seventeenth century. This tendency would result in inlays with landscape subjects on the altar of the Cappella dei Principi, a genre at that time not practised by local painters still tied to a

97. *Fame*, quadrilobe panel executed in Prague *c.* 1615–20, after a pictorial model probably supplied by the Florentine Bernardino Poccetti. Florence, Museo dell'Opificio delle Pietre Dure

98 and 99. Two table cabinets from the second decade of the seventeenth century. The first, with landscapes and fruit (the latter inspired by Florentine mosaics), was produced in Prague. Vienna, Kunsthistorisches Museum. The second, which combines flowers and birds with cartouches and geometric ornaments, was made by the Grand Ducal workshops in Florence. Ottawa, National Gallery

solid figurative tradition (Giusti 1978). Even the scenes from sacred history designed slightly later for the same altar set their scenes within broad landscape views, confirming the inclination to panoramic themes. Perhaps the still unidentified Nordic artist 'Emanuele the German' contributed models to their design (Przyborowski 1982). Florentine inlays of landscapes, though derived from pictorial models by diverse artists, betray in any case a common predilection for accurate and 'measurable' perspective scenes, following an essentially Tuscan taste, while Castrucci's panel of 1596 adopts a freer concept of space embraced in an aerial perspective. The latter characteristics lead one to conclude that at that date Cosimo was already perfectly established within the artistic-cultural context of Rudolf's court.

Attempts to distinguish Cosimo's hand from that of his son Giovanni among the many works from the first two decades of their workshop activity seem for the moment destined to be inconclusive (Giusti 1992; Distelberger 2002). This is because of the rarity of the works of certain provenance, the substantial cultural and stylistic continuity of Prague inlay work, and finally the probable impact of the assistants without whose collaboration one cannot explain such a vast production within the course of such a brief period. If one compares, for example, two panels of the same subject, the *Sacrifice of Isaac*, it is clear both that they belong to the same orbit and that there is a difference in quality that separates the two inlays. The first exhibits a composition as spatially complex as it is assured, bolstered by felicitous colour choices with brown and striped jaspers defining the steep and rocky cliff in the foreground, and a vibrant stippling of green and rose jaspers facilitating the gradual recession into depth of the waters and hills. On the other hand, the figures of the three protagonists, with the still distant angel that seems suspended in the air by moving clouds, are executed with a design maturity and subtlety of execution even in the minute incisions that define the lines of the face.

Whether or not this is a skilled work by Cosimo, as has been suggested (Distelberger 2002), it is certain that the second panel (ill. 95) presents a far more naive version of the same subject. This holds not only for the overall composition and the simplified execution, but also for the eloquent but ingenuously 'popular' poses of the figures, like the angel balanced on the tree. The other, larger panel offers a far different psychological tension and dialogue of glances between Jacob and the angel. The characteristics of this small work do not seem to owe much to Cosimo and even less to Giovanni Castrucci. More probably it was made by one of the less gifted assistants, on whom the two Florentines necessarily depended, also when making a *St Helen Adoring the Cross* on the small altar that was the Emperor's present for the Lobkowitz-Pernstein wedding of 1603 and which is equally modest compositionally and technically. Moreover, it cannot be excluded that on some occasions the less successful outcome of an inlay was due to the absence of an adequate pictorial

100

100. *The Banquet of Abraham*, designed in Florence by Bernardino Poccetti and translated into hardstone in Prague by the Castrucci workshop, *c.* 1610–20. Florence, Museo dell'Opificio delle Pietre Dure

101. *Landscape with Wayfarer*, executed in Prague in the second or third decade of the seventeenth century. Madrid, Museo del Prado

model. In fact in Prague, in contrast to Florence, original models were not worked up for inlays but the latter were instead inspired by existing works in the imperial collections, and preferably by prints of them because these were already graphic transpositions of the original painting and so facilitated the execution of the inlay.

In several cases it is possible to identify the roughly contemporary prints that the Castrucci workshop used. For example, the *View of Prague* (ill. 96) that appears in four different versions with small variations was derived from a print by Johannes Wechter of 1606 (Bukovinska 1988), itself reproducing a drawing by Philipp van den Bosch, active at the imperial court from 1604 to 1612. Giovanni Castrucci and his son and his grandson, with whom the Prague production of inlays ceased, was frequently inspired by the prints of Egid Sadeler

(1570–1629), the most important printmaker at the Prague court, which he made after fashionable landscapes by court artists such as Paul Bril and Pieter Stevens.

Elements of northern culture live alongside others derived from the Florentine manufacture in one of the most complete products of the Prague workshop, a rare table cabinet in ebony (ill. 98). With its front and sides clad with inlay panels inserted within a geometric framework, it belongs to a typology that may be dated to the last years of Cosimo's activity. A similar piece of furniture may date back to the same years (ill. 99) (González Palacios 1981). This is extremely close to the Prague object in the regular partitioning of its front and sides, and some of the inlay ornaments are very similar – for example the flowering stems and the quadrilobed cartouches in agate on the front of the Florentine cabinet are identical to those on the sides of the one executed in Prague. Perhaps, as some have hypothesized (Distelberger 1980), these floral panels came directly from Florence, since their design and palette of stones is typical of the Florentine inlays inspired by Ligozzi's naturalism.

But the mutual influences between the two workshops did not only travel in just one direction, as becomes clear from the emphasis that the central landscape oval acquired in Florence *studiolo*, there constructed with a view that extends into depth from a foreground bridge and tree-shadowed rocks, following the compositional models typical of Prague inlay landscapes. Direct examples of the latter cannot have been lacking in Florence, as we may see from a cabinet present in the Medici collections from at least 1624, and even though it was partially altered in nineteenth-century restorations, it

still conserves the structure and ingenuity typical of the famous ebonists of north-central Europe (Giusti 1978 and 1992). Within the *tempietto* architecture of this cabinet are twenty-four drawers and shutters, which can be opened by turning a jasper columnette on the façade, while two silver-gilt handles allow an ebony and ivory inlay tray (for backgammon) to slide out of the base. The hardstones that clad the façade and flanks are all Bohemian and Alsatian jaspers. Just as characteristic of Prague are the six inlay panels with architectural scenes within lake and river settings, in which the high terrain that encloses the horizon and the 'cubism' *avant la lettre* of the architecture find comparison with the oldest works by Castrucci, so much so that the cabinet may have been made in the first decade of the seventeenth century.

Confirming the frequency of the relations between the Florence and Prague workshops and the repute that Giovanni Castrucci enjoyed at the Medici court is the inlay of *The Banquet of Abraham* (ill. 100) commissioned from him in 1610 (Przyborowski 1982). This was intended to grace the foremost project of the manufacture in those days, the spectacular altar in hardstones for the Cappella dei Medici. Bernardino Poccetti created the pictorial model between 1606 and 1610, when it was sent to Prague and translated into an inlay finished in 1622, the same year it was consigned to the Florentine

102. *River View*, perhaps executed in Florence by Giuliano Pandolfini, formerly active in Prague, in the second quarter of the seventeenth century. Turin, Museo Civico

103. Detail of the central panel of a table in ebony and silver, signed by Hans G. Hertel and Lukas Kilian in 1626. Munich, Residenz

127
THE FORTUNES OF HARDSTONE INLAY IN
SEVENTEENTH-CENTURY EUROPE

104. Large table with landscapes and architectural 'caprices', inlaid with bands of silver and garnet, Castrucci workshop, third decade of the seventeenth century. Florence, Museo degli Argenti

105. Detail

court by Giuliano Pandolfini. The relevant document (Przyborowski 1982; also in *Splendori* 1988; Giusti 1978 and 1992) records that the work had been commissioned from Giovanni and finished (evidently after Castrucci's death in 1615) by his son Cosimo and his brother-in-law, the aforementioned Pandolfini. During the long production of the inlay, Poccetti's model, for which two preparatory drawings survive, underwent some modifications, as is evident from the figure of Abraham with his fur hat and fur-lined cape, perfectly suitable for a Bohemian noble but absolutely unthinkable in Florence. This is also the weakest part of the whole inlay in terms of execution, while the panel is instead superb in interpreting the three very elegant angel-wayfarers. One is tempted to attribute them to a third member of the Castrucci dynasty, Cosimo, author of the quadrilobe panel of *Fame* (ill. 97), whose impeccable execution enhances the stylized and Mannerist elegance of the figure (again probably based on a model executed in Florence) with the vivid and bright colours of the hardstones (Giusti 1978 and 1992).

The quadrilobe of *Fame*, perhaps conceived as the centre of an uncompleted tabletop, was only consigned to the Medici court in 1659 by the grandsons of Cosimo Castrucci, thirty years after manufacture had ceased in Prague. The final years, the 1620s and 1630s, had nonetheless seen creations of great quality, as two other inlays bound for Florence demonstrate, the product of collaboration between Cosimo Castrucci and his brother-in-law Giuliano Pandolfini, whose surname betrays a Florentine origin and who would conclude his own activity in Florence. In the inlays intended for Prague the landscape theme remained predominant whether as an exclusive subject or to set a religious scene, as in the *Holy Magdalene in Prayer* (ill. 94) which includes the sort of grand classicized ruins absent in Castrucci's older works but which recur throughout the late output of the workshop (Distelberger 2002). One of the most complete and skilful examples of this taste for ruins is the *River View* (ill. 102) in the Museo Civico of Turin, in which the unitary spatial vision and the calm pictorial rendering give the inlay such an Italianate tone that one might think that Pandolfini executed the work after his arrival in Florence and his entry into the Grand Ducal manufacture, where he is documented in the 1630s (Giusti 1992). A Florentine origin for the panel, which is otherwise typical of the Prague style, is also suggested by its later mounting in an ebony and gilt bronze frame, whose model and style show it must have been produced by the Medici workshops under Cosimo III (Massinelli in *Splendori*... 1988).

But the landscape type that is more typical of the late Prague style, and which consistently developed in the style of Cosimo and Giovanni, is the view in which a monumental and untamed mass of trees and rocks hangs over small buildings and the odd traveller, 'dissolving' into a gradually deepening background. A masterpiece in this genre is the great octagonal plaque (ill. 103) inserted at the centre of an ebony tabletop augmented by silver inlays, which belonged to the Elector of Bavaria and is signed by two Augsburg craftsmen in 1626, the year to which we might also date the Prague inlay (Heikamp in *Splendori*... 1988; Giusti 1992), although it is sometimes thought to be older (Distelberger 2002). Very similar in composition, with a painterly vibrancy, is the landscape (ill. 104) at the centre of a prestigious table entirely composed of hardstones, pre-

106. Seventeenth-century panel in Florentine-Prague style, in a large cabinet formerly in the British Royal collections. New York, private collection

107. Casket in gilt bronze and hardstones, executed in Prague in 1620–23. Vaduz/Vienna, collections of the Prince of Liechtenstein

108. Great tabletop executed by Giuliano Pandolfini in 1636 in Florence, on his return from Prague. Vaduz/Vienna, collections of the Prince of Liechtenstein

served in Florence and coming from the Medici collections (Giusti 1979 and 1992; Heikamp in *Splendori*... 1988).

Recently it has been suggested (Distelberger 2002) that this slab may have been made not long before the date of its first recorded appearance in Florence (1704), reutilizing stray pieces, perhaps the same as those attributed to Giovanni Castrucci in the imperial inventory of Prague. But the individual aspects and overall composition belong to a unitary and coherent conception, which may be ascribed to the Prague workshops, which were inactive after the 1630s. Moreover, the Florence table finds parallels in the last and excellent creations of the Prague workshops, beginning with the silver bands that border the inlays and mount small gems and garnets and which recur, though in this case using gilt bronze, in the aforementioned tabletop and cabinet (ill. 107) executed for Charles I of Liechtenstein.

This detail also confirms the fidelity of the Prague workshops to their originating stylistic motifs, for the motif of metallic bands with garnet inserts finds an early precedent in the famous table realized for Rudolf II by the Medici manufacture, which could have inspired the composition and subject matter of the Liechtenstein table. In the latter, there are also the landscapes of a Rudolfian taste, if not epoch, inspired by prints made a couple of decades earlier (Vincent 1985) and arranged in an orderly manner in rows parallel to the observer, which avoid those 'breakthrough' effects typical of the last Prague landscape views. Thus, alongside the favourite and shadily 'romantic' landscapes emerges another type of view, evident in both the Florence table and the Liechtenstein cabinet (ills. 104 & 107), with architectural 'caprices' of Italianate taste both in their subjects and their limpidly perspectival spatial organization.

Another theme, this time essentially abstract, that distinguishes the products of the Prague workshop throughout its history, and which are emphasized in the aforementioned Vienna cabinet and the Liechtenstein table, are the stereometric figures derived from the engravings of the *Perspectiva*

The Fortunes of Hardstone Inlay in Seventeenth-Century Europe

corporum regolarium of the great goldsmith Wenzel Jannitzer, published in Nuremberg in 1568. In this treatise the Platonic solids have become symbols of Renaissance cosmology, the tetrahedron for example representing fire, the octahedron air. The adoption of these images in Prague inlays is not therefore simply a decorative pretext, but reaffirms the capacity of hardstone artefacts to be 'microcosms' of the universe which de Boodt assigned to them in his treatise.

Nonetheless, other workshops also took up the theme of polyhedrons, which were striking and evocative even from a formal viewpoint, as a decorative motif. They appear, for example, in a Florentine cabinet of the late seventeenth century, that unites panels of views with ornaments in a style oscillating between Florence and Prague (Giusti 1992), particularly the geometric solids that assume a decorative function on the side panels clamping branches of flowers or supporting cups of fruit. Perhaps one may recognize in these cabinet inlays, whose front displays superb views of ruins (ill. 106), a product of the Florentine activity of Giuliano Pandolfini, who had arrived in Florence after the demise of the Prague workshops and whom Zobi (1857) cites as among the masters active in the Galleria dei Lavori under Ferdinando II. What is certain is that in 1636 Pandolfini created in Florence for Karl Eusebius of Liechtenstein (1611–84), the son of his former protector, a 'jasper' tabletop (ill. 108) that can be convincingly identified with the example still in the Liechtenstein collection, whose triumphal and naturalistic ornament blooms out of a black ground (Vincent 1985).

The overall design, probably conceived by a painter from the Medici circle, organizes the predominant floral theme within a network of cartouches, conches and cups of exuberantly late Mannerist taste, similar to the famous table being prepared for the Tribuna in the same years (ill. 72). Yet, other compositional motifs and techniques of execution of a more Bohemian stamp are grafted onto this Florentine basis. These would certainly have pleased the patron, whose heraldic arms occupy the quadrilobe at the table's centre, identical to the one that frames the *Fame* (ill. 97) inlay that Cosimo Castrucci had made in Prague. The two views that flank the coat of arms particularly recall the Prague style: the birds in the border cartouches resemble those on the two plaques in the Liechtenstein collection; the diffuse and skilful use of Bohemian jaspers confers a painterly vibrancy on elements of Ligozzian origin like the flowers, which the Florentine manufacture normally executed with stone slices of a single and contrasting colour.

A melange of elements derived from both Florentine and Prague practice is the basis for the productions of another European city that was to become a centre for marble inlay in the first half of the seventeenth century. In this case the production did not depend on royal commissions or recipients but the 'private' artistic workshops of Augsburg, the economic and cultural heart of Bavaria that, in the sixteenth century, would also blaze a trail in the vast and expert production of the decorative arts. Silverwork, ivory, jewelry, display furniture constructed with the most varied materials, and scientific and mechanical instruments were among the most sought-after specialities of the Augsburg workshops, which worked at full speed for the princely Wunderkammers of the whole of Europe, including naturally the Medici, and thereby encouraging a rich exchange of artistic ideas between Florence and Augsburg. It is necessary to ask, for example, whether the wooden cabinets which had already made

109. Inlay panels, decorating the internal façade of the 'German Cabinet'

110. The 'German Cabinet' executed by the Augsburg workshops between 1619 and 1626. Florence, Museo degli Argenti

Augsburg famous in the sixteenth century may not have influenced the oldest *studioli* produced by the Medici manufacture; similarly, to what degree the late sixteenth-century, naturalistic Florentine inlays, which often adopted the parrot on a branch as almost their distinctive logo, had borrowed the theme from Augsburg wood inlays, in which it already appears in the 1570s and 1580s (Giusti 1992). Nor can one be sure whether the 'gemmed carving' of the *ex-voto* (ill. 65) of Cosimo II reflected the influence of the extraordinary *Reliquary of St George*, similarly carved in hardstones encrusted with enamels and jewels and exhibited at the most important ceremonies in the Reiche Kapelle of the Elector of Bavaria. It had been in Augsburg in 1586–97, probably after a model of Friedrich Sustris, who had trained in Florence (Hojer-Stierhof-Heym 1995).

In Augsburg the circulation of ideas and artefacts found a strong node of activity in Philip Heinhofer (1578–1647), a multifarious individual who was an entrepreneur, art dealer, collector, intellectual and diplomat. After university in Padua, he had dedicated himself to art dealing from 1601, but in the meantime also undertook diplomatic missions for Henry IV of France and various German princes, establishing a network between the major courts of Europe, which would greatly favour his fortunes as an art dealer. In the free Lutheran city of Augsburg, where artistic production did not live off the impulses or under the protection of a princely court but arose out of multiple workshops, Heinhofer often assumed the role of a promoter. He produced especially sophisticated furnishings, which he designed and whose artisans he chose, and which he then 'placed' with a princely collector after first publicizing them by sending descriptions and drawings.

Cabinets that incorporated wondrous *naturalia* and *artificialia* in their external ornament and internal apparatus, small perfume boxes, travel chests and drug cabinets, tables and military chests were the preferred objects of Heinhofer's trade, and they were all distinguished by the studied ingenuity of their metamorphic structure, in which the Mannerist taste for the bizarre was married with the dictates of function. They were items that, as Heinhofer himself wrote, 'inside…were full of secrets and uses' (Heikamp 1966), like the mirror and travelling table which he offered for sale to Ferdinando II de' Medici in 1628, and whose interior concealed games, a travelling desk, drug cabinets, stools and even a table service and bed (Kriegbaum 1939). Unfortunately, all trace has been lost of this surprisingly versatile piece of furniture. In the same year, 1628, another amazing creation by Heinhofer arrived in Florence, the 'German Cabinet' (ill. 110), today in the Museo degli Argenti, given to the Grand Duke by the Archduke Leopold of the Tyrol, who had acquired it in 1626.

As monumental and complex as the great cabinet of Pomerania, formerly in Berlin, which Heinhofer produced between 1611 and 1616, the Florence cabinet also included two

111. Large cabinet in ebony, with internal façades in ivory and hardstones, Augsburg, around the middle of the seventeenth century. Paris, private collection

112. Detail

113. Detail of the high altar of Santa Corona, by the Corbarelli workshop, after 1681. Vicenza, church of Santa Corona

114. Detail of the high altar of Santa Giustina, by the Corbarelli workshop, second half of the seventeenth century. Padua, church of Santa Giustina

115. Detail of the altar of the Most Holy Sacrament, executed by the Corbarelli workshop in the second half of the seventeenth century. Padua, church of Santa Giustina

116. Tabletop with Minerva and *View of the Castle at Rheinfels*, hardstone inlay and relief, by the Florentine Francesco Mugnai for the Landgrave Karl of Hesse-Kassel, between the end of the seventeenth century and the first years of the eighteenth. Kassel, Landesmuseum

small landscapes in hardstones within a severe, octagonal block of ebony. Opening the cabinet revealed the marvels of its decoration and the collections concealed in its interior, inviting meditation on the relationship between nature, art and divinity, illustrated by the cabinet's decorations. The religious theme focused on the life of Christ, a wise choice since Heinhofer could never be sure during production whether the item in question was destined for a Catholic or Protestant prince. On the summit of the cabinet was a silver group of Christ, the Devil and Death, now lost. When the clock within the cabinet chimed, the figure of Christ stabbed the Devil with His cross and the eyes of Death teemed with snakes. Scenes and symbols of Christ are illustrated in more than two hundred hardstone plaquettes painted in oils, and their viewing might be accompanied by the sacred music played by an automatic organ concealed within the top of the cabinet. Next, if one wished to pass from contemplation to religious practice, one could extract an altar mensa from one shutter on the main façade, while all the necessaries for the liturgical service were placed in drawers with panelled hardstone fronts of birds on branches and landscape views.

These small inlays (ill. 109), of reduced dimensions and pleasing but not exceptional craftsmanship, demonstrate a good knowledge of Prague and Florence production: the 'truthful' depiction of small birds is based on the thoroughly naturalistic representations already in vogue at the end of the sixteenth century in Florentine inlay, while the landscape images of sun-drenched hills in Sicilian jasper (like those executed in the century's first decade for the altar in the Cappella dei Principi, ill. 51) alternate with views of towered hamlets in the style and materials of Prague inlays. Such 'imitations' were probably the work of the Augsburg workshops, which already cut hardstones in the sixteenth century and which were capable of experimenting in the new genre of stone inlay thanks to their free-ranging expertise. We can glean all this from a letter that Heinhofer sent to Rome in 1627, which boasts of 'two small works that those masters are producing at my expense, that is two inlay tables with beautiful stones...' (Heikamp 1966). That Heinhofer felt confident of the

117. *Karl, Landgrave of Hesse-Kassel*, inlay relief carved by Francesco Mugnai, beginning of the eighteenth century. Copenhagen, Rosenborg Castle

118. Great tabletop with polychrome inlays on a white ground, Grand Ducal workshops of Florence, first quarter of the seventeenth century. Paris, Jardin des Plantes, Galérie Mineralogique

quality of these two works is confirmed by his offer in the same year of a table to Ferdinando II de' Medici, a design for which survives. On this table, between silver fretwork inlays in the typical Augsburg style, were to figure inlay panels of parrots and bouquets of flowers on a black field in strict observance of the Ligozzi style.

The inlays with typically Florentine subjects of birds, flowers and flower vases held the field in Augsburg production anyway, without Heinhofer's artistic initiatives. They compose, for example, the decorations on a superb series of four cabinets in ivory (ill. 111) (Alfter 1986; Giusti 1992), all intended for royal collections, to which we may now add another example in the Sarti collection in Paris. The external structure of these table cabinets, mostly veneered in ebony, is of sober form and almost severe elegance in order to increase the 'wonderment' that the cabinet would excite once its twin shutters were opened. The façade and internal face of the two shutters are in fact veneered in ivory and hardstones, precious materials that the seventeenth century often loved to couple in ensembles whose physical sumptuousness married the ductile ingenuity of technique and the happy invention of the artistic design. The especially subtle workmanship and decorative motifs of the ebony parts, which combine a still Mannerist repertoire of small aedicules, volutes and urn-shaped vases in varied harmonies, seem to suggest that this group of cabinets originated in the workshop of Melchior Baumgartner (1621–96). Baumgartner was a specialist in ivory and the son of Ulrich Baumgartner, a famous cabinetmaker who had collaborated in Philip Heinhofer's most ambitious enterprises.

It was the practice of Baumgartner and the Augsburg workshops to create precious mixed-media ensembles that were the fruit of collaboration between diverse specialists, like, for example, the two ebony cabinets with lapis lazuli plaques and gilt bronze appliqués executed by Melchior Baumgartner for the Elector of Bavaria towards the middle of the century (Eikelmann 2002). It is therefore possible that an Augsburg workshop, which had mastered hardstone working, collaborated with Baumgartner on the cabinets with hardstone panels. As we have seen, hardstone carving and cutting had already been introduced into the city at the time of Heinhofer, and workshops were capable of producing excellent imitations of Florentine inlays. It cannot be excluded that the strong contacts with Florence also resulted in the acquisition of ready-made inlays that could then be mounted on furniture created in Augsburg. One may suppose this from certain inlays (ill. 112) on the Sarti cabinet, which are perfectly Florentine in their design, choice of stones and execution. Yet, on the whole the local production must have been of a good level, albeit devoid of any novelty and only proficient in copying Florence and Prague prototypes. This is demonstrated by a cabinet in the Royal Danish collection, whose eclectic combination of birds and flowers in the Ligozzi style with the polyhedrons characteristic of Castrucci also appear on the sides of a cabinet belonging to the same 'family', at Buckingham Palace (González Palacios 1981). All this raises reasonable doubt over whether the inlays normally attributed to Prague, which are too numerous for workshops that were active for only some thirty years and often applied to furnishings executed subsequently, can really all have been

119. Detail of the cabinet of Vittoria della Rovere, in ebony, gilt bronze and hardstones, executed in the Grand Ducal workshops towards 1680. Florence, Palazzo Pitti

120. Panel with floral subject, dated 1690, Grand Ducal workshops. Florence, Museo dell'Opificio delle Pietre Dure

121, 122 and 123. Three panels with themes in the style of Baccio del Bianco, fashionable in the inlays of the Grand Ducal workshops in the second quarter of the seventeenth century. Château de Versailles

made by the Castrucci. They may instead have been the fruit of that longer and more diffuse activity that characterized the workshops of Augsburg.

At the end of the century, in 1699, there came a limited but significant confirmation of the continuing German interest in Florentine manufacture of hardstones, when Cosimo III de' Medici granted the Landgrave Karl of Hesse-Kassel the services of Francesco Mugnai, a master in the Galleria dei Lavori. The Landgrave, a member of a family that had already esteemed and collected hardstone inlays in the sixteenth century, thus intended to emulate the initiative that great rulers had taken before him by instituting his own workshop as a direct 'branch' of the Florentine manufacture. The Landgrave continued this enterprise even after Mugnai's death in 1710. From a document of 1730 (Keysler 1756), the year of the Landgrave's death, we learn that the workshop had remained active until then, under the direction of 'Homagius…a man of great science and a proven mathematician', and employing artisans from Dresden (González Palacios 1981). These men were still working on a tabletop left incomplete twenty years earlier by Mugnai, who had coupled flat inlay with a relief mosaic in hardstones, following a practice rarely used by the Florence manufacture, the best example being the famous and extraordinary *ex-voto* of Cosimo II that we have mentioned several times (ill. 65).

The Kassel table (ill. 116) was left unfinished, probably because of the patron's death, and was completed in some parts with painted plaster. It remains an interesting work even though the eventual result does not match the original ambitions, perhaps also due to the modifications carried out during the long course of its execution. A travel journal of 1709 (von Uffenbach 1753) tells us that at the time Mugnai had been working for five years on the table, which foregrounds a Minerva in mosaic relief against a background of the castle at Rheinfels seen from the lake side. From this contemporary description, which praises the quality of execution of both the Minerva and the urban view, it is clear that Mugnai had already brought the work to a good point, and that all that was lacking was the expanse of water and the sky, for which the artist intended to use Bohemian jasper and an 'Italian stone', perhaps the chalcedony from Volterra, which Florentine craftsmen had often used to create clouds. Evidently local craftsmen completed these parts, which no longer correspond to the original intention, after Mugnai's death. They are, in fact, somewhat weak owing to the flat 'laying' of the Corsican jasper chosen for the water and the cut and rough grain of the stones that compose the unlikely sky. Nonetheless, there was a certain incongruence from the outset between the view in the grand oval, designed by the architect Prizier-Risse, and the border of bas-relief floral loops on a black ground that Mugnai conceived in the late baroque style in vogue at the Florence manufacture from which he came.

The importance accorded the carved parts of the table, and the technical mastery they reveal, make it clear that Mugnai must have been trained as a 'relief master', an activity that was quite distinct from the 'masters of flat inlay' in the virtuoso manufacture of Cosimo III. Confirmation comes from the majestic oval medallion (ill. 117), probably by Mugnai, that presents a half-length figure of the Landgrave dressed 'in heroic style' in a relief mosaic that emulates the mastery of Giovan Battista Torricelli, the major Florentine specialist in the glyptic arts, in its sculptural turning of form and refinement of engraving, which is particularly striking on the Landgrave's shimmering head of hair.

Outside the Germanic area, whose various centres were the protagonists of the hardstone arts through the seven-

124. *Parrot on the Branch of a Pear Tree*, seventeenth-century Florentine inlay, probably intended to clad a cabinet. Florence, Museo dell'Opificio delle Pietre Dure

teenth century and beyond, we must examine the laboratory of inlays and reliefs established by Louis XIV at the Gobelins. Even though its activity was limited in time and diffusion it remains of 'royal' standing. The initiative of the Sun King crowned an artistic and collecting tradition that had its distant roots in the fourteenth century, when France was among the few European areas to distinguish itself in hardstone carving, and found a new impetus during the sixteenth century thanks to Francis I's (1494–1547) ardent enthusiasm for Italian Renaissance art and the accession of Catherine de' Medici (1519–89) to the French throne. Catherine de' Medici shared the family passion for hardstones: she acquired vases carved by the Milanese workshops, but was also ready to accommodate the new art that was taking precedence over vases in hardstone caving, inlay tables in precious marbles. She even went to the lengths of obtaining the services of 'Il Franciosino', the major 'table master' who moved to Paris from Rome in 1579.

Rome continued to be the centre of reference for stone inlay in the early seventeenth century, although one may suppose that under Maria de' Medici, who included among her wedding gifts to Henry IV a portrait of the king in hardstone inlay (Giusti 1979), the works of the Florentine manufacture became better known at the French court. Richelieu nonetheless would continue to favour Rome in his sculpture and inlay acquisitions, amongst which was the famous table in the Galérie d'Apollon in the Louvre (González Palacios 1981). But it is under Cardinal Mazarin, who was extremely active both as a patron and collector of art, that the passion for stone inlays triumphed in the French court, to the degree that in 1657 the energetic prime minister planned to 'found a master-workshop' in Paris to be led by an artisan from Florence.

It is in these years, between 1654 and 1661, the year of his death, that the cardinal dedicated himself with particular fervour to reconstituting the personal collections that had been largely dispersed during the Fronde, and in which stone inlaid furnishings had occupied an important place. Mazarin's preferred advisor in this regard was the Florentine Abate Luigi Strozzi, to whom the cardinal addressed frequent and detailed requests, particularly for hardstone cabinets and, to a lesser extent, for tabletops. Perhaps one of the purchases from these years is the dazzling tabletop (ill. 118) with vases of flowers and birds on a white ground, also extraordinary in size, which entered the cardinal's collections between 1654 and 1661 (Saule 1982). In the stylized Mannerist elegance that still governs its naturalistic subject matter, it seems connected with the tastes of Ferdinando I de' Medici.

Preoccupied with obtaining quality works, at the right price, in 1659 Mazarin wrote to Strozzi 'so long as the work is beautiful, it is not necessary for them to come from the Galleria of His Highness: this prerogative serves no other purpose than to raise the price...' (Alazard 1924). This seems to confirm something that is to date insufficiently clear from Florentine documents, namely that during this period the craftsmen of the Grand Ducal manufacture were creatively and commercially 'moonlighting', and that in the shadow of the exclusive Galleria dei Lavori there also operated private workshops capable of imitating its style.

The routine that Mazarin established with Strozzi and with Florence was followed by Colbert, who in 1661 ordered for Louis XIV a pair of tables, which he emphasized should be 'the most beautiful and of the best invention that one can imagine...these things must be greater than ordinary and more exquisite both in terms of delicacy of work and in terms of their form, which must be singular.' Grandiosity of effect and technical perfection: here, in synthesis, are the declared criteria that inspired the taste of Louis XIV, whose desire for originality is also manifest in the proposal that the design for the flowers to adorn the two tables made in Florence should be sent from Paris, and in the rejection soon after of some designs for cabinets sent by an unidentified Florentine artist, '...a man who is assuredly brilliant and capable, but the bizarreness of their forms was not at all pleasing'.

Plans progressed to create an artistic workshop worthy of the first court in Europe, enlisting the best craftsmen that France could offer and importing the specializations that had been developed elsewhere, such as the '*ouvrage de Florence*' (or Florentine inlay), to which end three specialists were brought over from Florence. The year after the foundation of the Gobelins, established in 1667, the representative of the French court to the Medici was charged with the recruitment. The same year, 1668, a small équipe moved to France, headed by Ferdinando Migliorini, a 'master in relief' from the rolls of the Grand Ducal manufacture, and accompanied by his brother Orazio and Filippo Branchi. Two years later they were joined by Gian Ambrogio Giachetti, who also came from the Galleria dei Lavori and would die in 1709, the last of a Florentine team that for thirty years constituted the small but creative hardstone workshop of the Sun King (González Palacios 1981, 1988, 1996).

Given the 'Florentineness' of the workshop, which could only count on French help during the first and final periods of its activity, and the success that Florentine inlays continued to find at the French court, it is not surprising that the works that came out of the Gobelins maintained fairly strict ties with their Florentine prototypes, even while pioneering fresh stylistic and expressive modes on more than one occasion. The result was a few original works, though not of the unitary and varied appearance of the inlays that had been made in Prague. In short, there was no real 'Gobelins style' that can be identified in the hardstone inlays and reliefs produced for the Sun King, perhaps because their design was entrusted to diverse artisans whose acquaintance with the art of *pietra dura* remained intermittent.

This does not diminish the fact that, during the extremely long activity of the workshop, from 1669 until the first decade of the eighteenth century, many prestigious works were produced inspired by those criteria of 'magnificence, capability, richness and grandeur' that were as much the foundation of his programme of government as they were the many artistic, political and social initiatives of the Sun King. Today what impedes us from fully understanding the hardstone furnishings of this epoch is the fact that, even if they did not disappear altogether, many were often dismembered due to rapid changes in taste. Already at the time of the Regency, the imposing and sumptuously mixed-media furniture of the *grand siècle* had fallen out of favour, not to mention the conceptual and theoretical complexity of hardstone inlays. Conversely and thanks to another revolution in French eighteenth-century taste, the avant-garde of Europe in the field of the decorative arts and furniture, many of the inlay panels in

125. Tabletop with animals, the royal arms and the monogram of Louis XIV, made at the Gobelins. Paris, Musée du Louvre

126. Detail

hardstones by the Gobelins have survived because they were reutilized in furnishings in the era of Louis XVI.

Only two majestic cabinets remain as testimony to the magnificence of hardstone furnishings under Louis XIV. They were released from the royal collections in 1751 and are today at Alnwick Castle, but were recorded in the King's apartments in 1694 (Setterwall 1959). In architectural furniture, rather than the micro-architecture that characterized even the most imposing Florentine cabinets of the period, the wooden elements were realized by Domenico Cucci, who had already worked for Cardinal Mazarin. Cucci may also have executed the extremely rich gilt bronze ornaments, including the monogram of Louis XIV on the façade and those framing the fourteen hardstone panels that had been made at the Gobelins under the direction of Migliorini.

One also observes the presence of elements in the Florentine style and others in a more original style, the poles between which Gobelins production seemed to oscillate. The pair of lake scenes in the upper register suggest a direct

125

126

'import' from Florence, such is their fidelity in subject and expressive style to the views that had come back into fashion at this moment in the Medici workshop and which find their first application on the cabinet of Vittoria della Rovere (ill. 119), of around 1680 (Giusti 1979). The four bottom panels also betray Florentine models, with the bird resting on boughs of fruit bound by a curling ribbon, a canonical motif in baroque Medicean inlays, but here the mottled stones render it 'impressionistic', a taste that seems to characterize the flat inlays of the Gobelins as opposed to the Florentine predilection for brightly coloured patterns and sharp chiaroscuro.

This use of stone with vibrant and almost fluid nuances becomes more evident in panels where the subject also aspired to its own originality, highlighting isolated animals against naturalistic backgrounds. This does not mean that Florence lacked inlays with animal subjects, which had already been produced in the first half of the century, but rather that these were normally vivacious 'maquettes' intentionally simplified and detached from their context, while the Gobelins inlays make animal themes true and proper portraits, which are then amplified by the natural context in which they are set. Analogous subjects were fashionable in the same years in the famous tapestry manufacture of the Sun King, following cartoons of both French and Dutch painters such as Jacques Carrey and Pieter Boel, who could have also been the authors of the models for the inlays. Certain oil paintings and drawings by Boel, which focus on representing a single animal, are similar to the stone inlays made by Florentine craftsmen (González Palacios 1988).

The preponderance of these subjects in Gobelins production is confirmed by four drawings made by the architect Robert de Cotte, which should perhaps be interpreted less as models than copies after tabletops (González Palacios 1996). Two of them survive. On a table today in the Louvre, the heraldry of Louis XIV and portraits of birds share the tabletop 'democratically', perhaps as homage to the royal passion for hunting, to which the other table at Compiègne may also allude with its woodland animals in the company of the goddess Diana. Both tables are partitioned into discrete panels. In the Compiègne version these panels are superimposed, with a certain incoherency, on the vegetal tangle of the background, while in the Louvre example (ill. 125) they are arranged into a tighter concatenation. It is possible, as has been suggested (González Palacios 1988), that this type of composition with distinct panels, which also recurs in the two other drawings of lost tables, was the by-product of the practice of proceeding by single elements, rather than an intentionally unified ensemble, whether in design or execution. Another reason to reach this conclusion is that the two panels with ducks inserted into the Louvre table also figure, as detached items, in the list of inlays in Ferdinando Migliorini's studio at his death in 1683. This method of pro-

ceeding by single elements, which was used in Florence for cabinets or caskets but not for tabletops, perhaps originated in the need to capitalize on the tiny team of Gobelins inlayers, since unitary and complex designs required the collaboration of several artisans, and which was only possible with the tens of employees working for the Medici workshop.

The exuberant Louvre tabletop (ill. 127) was instead of unitary conception and execution. Luxuriant spokes of flowers, lyres and cups of fruit radiate from its central cartouche and the heraldic fleurs-de-lis of France occupy its four corners. Even though the correspondence with the Abate Strozzi speaks of several tables made in Florence in the early years of Louis XIV's reign to designs sent from Paris, it seems more likely that this tabletop was executed at the Gobelins

127. Tabletop with the heraldic lilies of France, made at the Gobelins. Paris, Musée du Louvre

128. Panel with hardstone relief, from the Gobelins, period of Louis XIV, reused to decorate the central zone of a later cabinet, in the style of Adam Weisweiler. Stockholm, Royal Palace

(Alcouff 1981; González Palacios 1988; Giusti 1992). It would probably not have remained such an anomaly in their repertoire if the many other tables manufactured there, particularly between 1687 and 1699, had survived.

The idea of a unitary composition and the varied and intense palette seem indebted to Florentine prototypes, but the choice of vibrant and 'mottled' stones is characteristic of the Gobelins, because they softened the forms and made them less harsh than Florentine inlays. In this respect a comparison with the different rendering of subjects common to the Louvre table and Florentine inlays, such as parrots and verdure, may prove significant. The Louvre table is unusual and skilful both in choosing the nuances of the striking slabs of sardonyx and in their mounting. They suggest the hemispherical body of cups, supported by lions' paws and a central pine-cone, a decorative motif that was common on other courtly furnishings of the time, as well as some Boulle furniture (González Palacios 1988). Also and above all distinctively French is the crowded decoration of the piece, albeit governed by a classical clarity, which reappears in some contemporary cartoons of the Savonnerie (Giusti 1992).

The two cabinets at Alnwick and the three tables examined here constitute for the moment our total knowledge of 'genuine' Gobelins production, since all other known works are *disiecta membra* of dismantled furniture, reused as individual elements on furnishings of the neoclassical era (see next chapter). A commode by Adam Weisweiler (ill. 168) at Buckingham Palace incorporates inlay panels of floral subjects, amongst which the central one stands out for its compositional richness and departure from Florentine prototypes, with its fruit basket surmounted by a parrot and inspired by some contemporary still life.

Yet another cup of fruit with birds, but this time in mosaic relief, decorates the great panel at the centre of a cabinet in the Weisweiler style (ill. 128) and it is among the most admirable products of the Gobelins in the sensuous rounding of its carving and the splendidly polished gamut of stones. Draped around the plinth supporting the cup with muscular softness is a festoon of fruit, a motif from classical tradition widely used in Louis Quatorze decorations, also fashionable at the Medici manufacture in the same period, and always with the fruit blooming from leafy tendrils of bronze. Even though the French court had excellent bronze casters, fruit festoons, which recur in a piece of furniture at Buckingham Palace and on a cabinet in the Wallace Collection, were also popular at the Gobelins, where the motif increased the fascinating naturalistic evocation of the subject by the exclusive use of hardstones as materially tactile as they were intangible. Indeed it was probably this very quality that would prove unappealing to the lightness of the emerging rococo style, which spurred on the end of hardstone working at the Gobelins, though not its disappearance from French art.

129. Florentine inlay from the Grand Ducal workshops, intended for the façade of a cabinet, about the middle of the seventeenth century. Florence, Museo dell'Opificio delle Pietre Dure

CHAPTER 5

SPLENDOURS OF THE ANCIEN RÉGIME

For the entire seventeenth century the Medici manufacture in Florence was the common base in Italy and abroad for the artistic development of work in hardstones. And, although it began to witness a decline in the first decades of the eighteenth century, it still remained a vital centre. Just as the firework displays in which the baroque era revelled always closed with some gloriously explosive finale, so Cosimo III de' Medici prodigally distributed among the courts of Europe the creations of his Galleria dei Lavori, the splendid symbols of a Medici dynasty on the point of extinction.

Moreover, in that area of Germany that had already proven itself sensitive to the fascination of Florentine mosaics, we witness yet another episode directly influenced by them: the *Florentiner Zimmer* in the Schloss Favorite at Förch near Rastatt (Przyborowski 1998). This palace was constructed between 1710 and 1712 by the Margravine of Baden-Baden, Sibyl Augusta (1675-1737), widow of the Margrave Ludwig-William and the Duchy's ruler until her son came of age. She divided her energies between the sumptuous court life of the era and a life of ardent devotion. Indeed, it was perhaps the Margravine's remorse for such worldly pomp that induced the self-critical epitaph that she requested for her tomb: 'Pray for the great sinner.'

Certainly there was nothing modest about the design or the cost of the Florentine 'cabinet' (ill. 130) that Sibyl Augusta commissioned to be her son's audience room at Rastatt. The project included revetments of 758 panels, in which Florentine inlays alternated with mirrors, painted glass, glass mosaic, scagliola, paintings on agate and mother-of-pearl intarsia. This complex work was begun in the second decade of the eighteenth century. In 1723 part of the inlays had already arrived from Florence, but final retouching and completion of the room, which also vaunted a pavement in scagliola and a dado with lacquered paintings, are documented between 1732 and 1739, by which point the Margravine had died. Sibyl Augusta had enjoyed direct and personal relations with the Florentine court thanks to her sister Anna Maria Francesca, who had married Cosimo III's heir Gian Gastone, and in 1719 the Margravine had also made a brief visit to the city. Following this trip the Grand Duke sent her the gift of a wall plaque with an admirable *Annunciation* (ill. 131), based on the antique fresco venerated in Florence, which the manufacture had often replicated with ever more fantastic bronze and hardstone ornaments. The version sent to the Margravine in 1720 was executed under the

130. The *Florentiner Zimmer* in the summer palace of Favorite, clad with Florentine inlays, third and fourth decades of the eighteenth century. Rastatt, Schloss Favorite

131. *Annunciation*, wall plaque executed in 1720 by the Grand Ducal workshops of Florence. Karlsruhe, Badisches Landesmuseum

direction of Foggini and with the participation of the inlayer Francesco Borghese (González Palacios 1981, II; idem. 2001).

Rastatt probably owes its collection of Florentine inlay panels to the same contacts, just as the very idea for such unusual *boiserie* must have been suggested to the Margravine by some rooms in the Palazzo Pitti that have since been destroyed but were then clad in hardstones. By 1723, a few years after her Florentine sojourn, a good number of the inlay panels had already arrived at Rastatt. Today they number 85 pieces, of which 55 revet the room, 15 compose its central table, and another 15 adorn the altar in the court chapel. The only religious theme among the inlays inserted into this scagliola altar frontal is the *Annunciation*, again inspired by the celebrated Florentine fresco, while the other panels portray flowers, views and baskets of fruit, subjects typical of the baroque repertoire of Grand Ducal inlays (ill. 132). The same themes return in the wall inlays of the *Florentiner Zimmer*, some of which probably come from the Florentine manufacture, where stocks of panels were kept for cabinets, jewel boxes and similar items (ill. 133). These were often executed in anticipation of later use on wooden furnishings, which did not always end up incorporating all the panels that the Grand Duke's industrious craftsmen had prepared.

Other inlays instead display a more modern taste and were probably created *ad hoc* for the Margravine. In many cases they are fantastic landscapes – a subject fashionable for inlays since they had been used in Florence on a furnishing of regal pomp, the cabinet of the Grand Duchess Vittoria della Rovere (ill. 119), in around 1680 (*Splendori...* 1988). The 'small views' of Rastatt, both picturesque and captivating in the slightly naive simplicity of their compositions, become more complex and structured in the three ovals of the della Rovere table where the Florentine intarsia is combined with mother-of-pearl inlays, in the style that the Augsburg workshops had already made popular in the previous century.

Three still-life inlays in the wall panelling are also inspired, like the views, by seventeenth-century painting (ill. 134). The still-life genre was fairly unusual for Florentine inlays, especially the 'laid table' type that was so common in painting. To my knowledge, in fact, the latter subject only appears at Rastatt and in one other panel. Equally rare, although a cabinet at Frederiksborg and twin cabinets at the castle of Ligne in France offer some parallels, is the only mythological theme to appear among the panels, a *Centaur* (ill. 135) of beautiful design and carefully chosen colours. On the other hand,

132. Altar frontal, with Florentine inlays, early eighteenth century, Grand Ducal workshops. Rastatt, Court Chapel

133. Detail of a Florentine inlay with a floral theme, comparable with panels in the *Florentiner Zimmer* at Rastatt. Florence, Museo dell'Opificio delle Pietre Dure

134. Eighteenth-century tabletop, with assembly of Florentine landscapes and naturalistic themes. Rastatt, Schloss Favorite, Florentiner Zimmer

135. Wall panel with *Centaur*, a mythological theme recurrent in Medicean inlays between the late seventeenth and early eighteenth centuries. Rastatt, Schloss Favorite, Florentiner Zimmer

136. Detail of a wall panel with *Still Life*, of a type unusual in the Medici manufacture. Rastatt, Schloss Favorite, Florentiner Zimmer

manufacture inlays from the first half of the seventeenth century had included at least one subject from ancient myth among their figurative motifs, which continuously diminished in number compared with naturalistic themes as the century progressed. The subject was Orpheus bewitching the animals with his music. It is probable that an engraving by Antonio Tempesta (1555–1630) contributed to the success of this theme in Florentine inlays at the time of Cosimo II. Indeed, scenes of Orpheus the musician (ill. 138) decorate the central shutter of more than one cabinet, of varying technical quality but all derived from a similar pictorial source (González Palacios 1993). Finally, Orpheus even appears in an inlay panel of great design and technical accomplishment, on the throne of the Red Fort at Delhi (Koch 1988), which still arouses as much surprise and admiration as the mythical musician did among his beastly audience.

Yet, beyond the few subjects at Rastatt that attest to the Margravine's taste for more innovative and unusual subjects in Florentine inlay, it is clear that in the last phase of the Grand Ducal manufacture the *ancien goût* – as it was defined by the manufacture's director during the Napoleonic period – remained predominant: that is, 'to represent grotesques and flowers on a background of black marble.' This does not mean that the tables that Cosimo III sent as gifts to Frederick IV of Denmark in 1709 (González Palacios 1986), to Frederick Augustus of Saxony in 1713 (Przyborowski 1998), or to the Elector of Bavaria in 1716 (González Palacios 1986) were not still the prodigious fruits of a great artistic tradition. In all of them the plumage of birds and petals enflames the nocturnal brilliance of the background. In fact, not only did this schema continue into the less unsparing but still inspired production of the final reign of Gian Gastone de' Medici (ill. 139), but it also survived the reorganization and new creative direction of the manufacture on its passage into the hands of the new dynasty of Habsburg-Lorraine, in 1737.

The court manufacture awaited and lived through this moment in great trepidation. Even if it was no longer as well manned as it had been during the seventeenth century, in 1720 the manufacture still numbered nine 'workshops' employing numerous craftsmen, six of them directed by 'relief masters' and three by 'masters of flat inlay'. Francesco Ghinghi (1689–1762), a specialist in carving the hardstone reliefs especially prized by the late baroque taste for plasticity, narrates in a few well-chosen words the fateful events in his manuscript *Autobiography* of 1753 (González Palacios 1997 and 1993): In 1737 'Gian Gastone, Grand Duke of Tuscany, passed

164
SPLENDOURS OF THE *ANCIEN RÉGIME*

137

137. *View of Sailors on a Coast*, panel of 1730 given shortly after to the Habsburg-Lorraines, new Grand Dukes of Tuscany. Vienna, Kunsthistorisches Museum

on to a better life...last Ruler of the Royal House of Medici, *true and legitimate patrons of all the virtues and Noble Arts*. Now that they were lost to practitioners in the fine art of working hardstones, their foundation and support declined to such a point that these practitioners were reduced to the final extremes of perdition....' Ghinghi's nostalgic tribute to the Medici sounds all the more convincing because it was written fifteen years after the event, and because Ghinghi and another nine artisans from the manufacture had entered the service of the King of Naples, Charles III of Bourbon, at his invitation in the same year, 1737.

As the new Grand Duke of Tuscany, Francis Stephen of Lorraine (r. 1737–65), was the consort of the Empress Maria Theresa of Austria, he continued to reside in Vienna and made only one visit to his Grand Duchy in 1739. The absence of a court in Florence and a more parsimonious regime made serious inroads into the artistic legacy of the Medici, both in terms of possessions and enterprises. Thus, before too long the glorious Medici Tapestry Works, which had also been founded in the sixteenth century, ceased production. A different fate awaited the manufacture of hardstones, however. Thanks to its internationally recognized supremacy and the strong naturalistic inclinations of the new Grand Duke, who still managed to pay it a visit even in his brief Florentine sojourn, the manufacture was able to maintain its antique traditions under the new name of the 'Imperial and Royal Establishment for Works in Hardstones'. Certainly the reorganization of the workshop, which was doubly necessary owing to the administrative laxness of the last Medici, abided by economic criteria that could not fail to influence the consistency and rhythm of production. Indeed, it would never again reach the levels of the Medici, although the quality of the products was still guaranteed by abundant stockpiles and practised expertise of the craftsmen.

As for the unfinished and grandiloquent Cappella dei Principi (ill. 42), which now also became the mausoleum of the new dynasty, only its external walls were completed and the proud challenge of its founder, Ferdinando I de' Medici, to clad it throughout with hardstones was shelved. The hardstones would have crept up the walls from the pavement and then spread across the great dome, which had been planned as a surreal, nocturnal vault of lapis lazuli, spangled with gilt bronze rosettes.

In the first Lorrainese phase the manufacture generally preferred creations of exquisite taste but reduced commitment, all of them destined for the Viennese court and mostly pursuing the floral repertoire of late baroque tradition, albeit with a certain graphic caprice of rocaille flavour. But an inlay panel of *View of Sailors on a Coast* (ill. 137), given by the new Grand Duke to his father-in-law the Emperor of Austria in 1739, introduces a new compositional flair and studied chromatic awareness into the landscape themes that had become

138

customary under Cosimo III in small pictures and panels. Such panels had enjoyed Europe-wide diffusion, as the aforementioned case of Rastatt attests. What most likely contributed to this popularity was Cosimo III's concession to the manufacture's masters, in the last years of his reign, of the right to work for themselves in their free time for private buyers. The latter were in large part wealthy and much solicited visitors to Florence who were more than happy to procure small but nonetheless excellent samples of the Medicean craftsmen's skill (Przyborowski 1998).

View of Sailors on a Coast, now in Vienna, instead aimed at the characteristics of a true and proper painting, and its model was a seascape painted by the Dutch artist Jacob de Heusch (Distelberger 2002). Indeed, it forecasts a revolution in the repertoire and style of Florentine inlays that would soon become programmatic. Nor is it coincidental that this revolution immediately followed the nomination of the Frenchman Louis Siriès (c. 1686–1766) as manufacture director. Siriès had entered its employ as a goldsmith under Cosimo III, in 1722, and was to be followed in this office by three generations of Siriès who guided the manufacture's production until the bitter end of the Grand Duchy of Tuscany.

Before moving definitively to Florence, Louis Siriès had lived in Paris, working for the French court with the title of 'goldsmith to the King'. His training in an environment that was then in the avant-garde of European artistic taste probably allowed Siriès to free himself from the slightly old-fashioned subjects of 'grotesques and flowers' (ill. 76), which had been the basis of Florentine inlay for more than a century, and substitute them with 'panels representing buildings enriched by landscapes and figures'. So says his great-grandson, Carlo Siriès (d. 1854), in a manuscript *Memoir* of 1808, which attributes his forebear with the merit for this innovation and which is borne out by contemporary testimony (Pelli 1766–73).

Although Louis Siriès personally cultivated the glyptic arts, carving especially prized cameos for Maria Theresea (Giulianelli 1753; Kris 1929), he set aside the sculptural tradition in hardstones that had been counted among the glories of the Galleria during the baroque era, and the fantastic forms in which it had been expressed. Instead, Siriès concentrated on producing flat inlays, wall-mounted panels in particular, which he intended, as his contemporary Pelli writes: 'to be far better, using better quality, better taste, correct design, good gradation and harmony in the colour of the stones.'

To ensure this enterprise enjoyed the artistic dignity that had always distinguished the manufacture's production, Siriès now needed an artist of quality. Unfortunately, after the death of the brilliant Foggini (1725) the Galleria dei Lavori could no longer count on artists of proven talent to dedicate themselves systematically to the designs of hardstone panels. Therefore, Siriès sought artistic collaboration with an emergent artist on the Florentine scene, Giuseppe Zocchi (1711–67), to guarantee the renaissance in themes and style that he planned for Florentine inlays. In 1750, after a trial year, Zocchi became permanent creator of pictorial models for the manufacture, a post that he maintained happily until his death (Giusti 1979; González Palacios 1986; Tosi 1997).

Onto a Florentine training, based on solid design, Zocchi grafted his knowledge of Venetian *vedutismo* and its lively curiosity about contemporary society. He was just as inspired by luminaries of classicized *capricci* and picturesque views, such as Giovanni Paolo Pannini (1691–1765) and Joseph Vernet (1714–89), to whom the young artist had become close during a fruitful stay in Rome. Zocchi's unquestionable talent to reproduce the fashionable themes of contemporary pictorial culture now offered Siriès the best possibility of revivifying that 'painting in stone' which had been one of the objectives of the manufacture's founder, Ferdinando I de' Medici. However, the new motivation underlying Siriès's decision was probably a classicist conviction in the supremacy of painting as the primary art form. Yet, the consequent risk that hardstone inlay might lose its expressive autonomy was avoided thanks to the master-carvers' ability to exploit the almost infinite pictorial potential of the stones themselves.

Between 1750 and 1767, the year of his death, Zocchi executed more than sixty models in oils, in series of two to six subjects, alternating between views of ruins and landscapes (ills. 140 & 141), genre and costume scenes, and above all the allegorical subjects that pleased the didactic tastes of the age. The manufacture spent almost twenty years executing these models for Francis Stephen of Lorraine and they were all planned to fill his palace in Vienna, which would thus become a unique 'gallery in stone', laid out to a system as much Enlightenment as Habsburg in style. Today this 'gallery' survives almost intact at the Hofburg, to which it was transferred at the end of the eighteenth century.

Missing are four panels that represent the *Five Senses* as elegant *plein air* allegorical subjects, completed in 1752 and

138. Cabinet decorated at the centre with an inlay of *Orpheus*, surrounded by animals on other panels, Grand Ducal workshops, c. 1620. Detroit, Institute of Art

139. *Parrot*, panel given by Gian Gastone de' Medici to the Elector of Saxony, and still bound to the naturalistic repertoire of the seventeenth century. Dresden, Grünes Gewölbe

141

given by the Empress of Austria to Catherine II of Russia (1729–96). Catherine II admired the panels so much that she had them mounted in the centre of the four walls of the Amber Room at Tsarskoye Selo (now Pushkin) – finished in 1770 – as 'tuning forks' for the material sumptuousness of the surrounding room. The subsequent fate of these four inlays, once believed to have been lost during the Second World War, was also unusual. In recent years the panel representing *Smell* reappeared in Germany and was returned to its Russian home. During the reconstruction of the Amber Room, inaugurated in 2003, a small team of craftsmen succeeded in resuscitating the difficult art of inlay on Russian soil, using Zocchi's original models to make more than worthy hardstone replicas.

Yet, the *Five Senses* were not the only Florentine inlays to arrive in distant and regal Russia. It is still unclear how and when a hardstone *View of the Port of Livorno* arrived in the Baths next to the palace constructed and furnished with exquisite classicized taste by Robert Cameron for Catherine II. Again it followed one of Zocchi's models, one of a series of four views

140. The hardstone version of the *Allegory of Air* by Giuseppe Zocchi. Vienna, Hofburg

141. *Allegory of Air*, model painted by Giuseppe Zocchi in 1750. It inaugurated a series of over sixty hardstone panels made in Florence for the Viennese court. Florence, Museo dell'Opificio delle Pietre Dure

142. *View of the Port of Livorno*, hardstone panel after a model by Giuseppe Zocchi of 1761–62. Vienna, Hofburg

140

of Livorno painted in 1762. Today this inlay languishes in the palace stores, but formerly it hung beside the entrance to the Agate Studio. Here it emphasized the jewelled appearance of a room swathed in a decor alluding to Pompeian 'encaustic' but in reality fashioned from slabs of green and red jasper from the Urals.

This *View of the Port of Livorno* was the second hardstone replica after Zocchi's model, and not a gift (like the *Five Senses*) to the Russian crown from the panels sent to Vienna. For the same view is included in the *Four Views of the Port of Livorno* that arrived in Vienna shortly after Zocchi had prepared their models in 1762 (ill. 142) (Giusti 1979; Distelberger 2002).

It was, furthermore, not unusual for the Florence manufacture to produce replicas of their most successful inlays. This was the case with the panel of *Architecture*, which was reproduced for an unknown but undoubtedly illustrious recipient in 1754, the same year that had seen the execution of *The Four Arts* for the Emperor of Austria after models made by Zocchi in 1752–53 (González Palacios 1986). Zocchi illustrated the allegory of the Liberal Arts, a theme that was susceptible to excessive solemnity if not outright pomposity, with captivating *tranches de vie* that seem to be drawn from the graceful and acute portrayals of contemporary Venetian society by Pietro Longhi (1782–85). The decision to reject Zocchi's earlier, more 'realistic' inventions were, if anything, occasioned by the more classicist and slightly academic tastes of Siriès, to whom Zocchi had to submit the preparatory sketches for every painting for approval and correction.

Such corrections are apparent in the panel of *Painting*. The preliminary sketch vivaciously represents a painter's studio, in which Zocchi's agile line with slightly ironic curiosity describes the mannequin pieces hanging from a wall, the disorder of the overturned easels, and an antique head that democratically shares a shelf with soiled paint pots. All these details were drastically eliminated from the final model and the corresponding inlay (ill. 143), which transforms the vivacity of the early and cordial idea into a courtly, classical scene.

143. *Painting*, hardstone panel from the series of *The Four Arts*, after a model by Giuseppe Zocchi of 1752–53. Florence, Museo dell'Opificio delle Pietre Dure

144. Tabletop with hunting scene and gentlemen on horseback. Florentine inlays from the second half of the eighteenth century. Berlin, Schloss Friedrichsfelde, Stiftung Stadtmuseum

145. Panel with a *Figure of a Lady*, executed by the Florence manufacture at the end of the eighteenth century. Florence, Museo dell'Opificio delle Pietre Dure

The same happened to the model for the *Sculpture*, in which the polished Apollo to which the sculptor makes the final touches substitutes a shapeless statue barely roughed out, which the original design intended to summarize the idea of an artist's work in progress.

Whatever the case, the sixty-eight hardstone panels executed between 1750 and 1765 were dispatched in quick succession to Vienna, at a rate of extraordinary speed given the quantity and quality of the endeavour. Zocchi's models in oils remained at the manufacture in Florence. Detached from comparison with their hardstone versions, which were literally dazzling in the splendour of their materials and the skill of their execution, it is easier to appreciate the elegant composition and felicitous pictorial spontaneity of their author. The success of the series created from his models, which many visitors saw in execution, above all French and Englishmen who included Florence and its exceptional manufacture as an obligatory stop on the Grand Tour, is attested by the vast European diffusion of small inlay panels containing a single and elegant figure dressed in the fashion of the time (ill. 145) (González Palacios 1988). In these graceful products the manufacture exploited the ability to render 'figure subjects', which it had acquired preparing the complex panels for Vienna. The small panels, for which cartoons were sometimes reused but colour schemes normally changed, were probably produced as individual items. It is in this form, in fact, that they have normally come down to us, though they could also be easily mounted in series on cabinets and tabletops, which themselves survive in subtle copies.

In the decade following Zocchi's death (1767) the Florentine manufacture chose a new direction in hardstone inlay under the guidance of the dynamic Siriès family, themselves artists attentive to developments in European taste in the applied arts. Under the influence of the emerging neo-classical style, inlays now took as their subject not 'works in imitation of figurative painting', but an 'ornamental painting' focused on an unprecedented and sophisticated repertoire of still lifes.

Zocchi, it must be said, had also made fruitful advances in this direction when he designed, between 1760 and 1765, two console tops, destined as usual for Vienna. These displayed no figures but rather drew their exquisite decorative value from two striking garlands, one of flowers and butterflies, the other of shells, coral and pearls (ill. 146) (Giusti 1979). Bowing to the didactic tastes then fashionable in the Enlightenment court of Vienna, these subjects were conceived as allegories of water and air, although such symbolism only supplied the pretext for the seductive inventiveness of two festoons that could skilfully follow the curved profiles of the consoles. Zocchi was an artist open to the most diverse influences but well rooted in Florentine pictorial tradition. On this occasion he seems to have recalled the pictorially evocative and naturalistically perceptive version that the painter Bartolomeo Bimbi (1648-1730), a still-life specialist much admired in Medici Florence, had given to a composition of 'marine subjects' and shells in a large painting now in Siena (Gregori 2002). Zocchi, for his part, alleviated its Seicento naturalism with a rococo but never precious capriciousness, which the inlay masters were able to render in stone with apparent facility and extraordinary felicity in two tabletops, now divided between Vienna and Paris (González Palacios 1986; Giusti 1992).

Both were originally conceived to stand out in the Viennese palace of the Grand Duke's brother, Peter Leopold (1747-92), who ruled Florence from 1765 on. The console top with shells, once supported by a siren (now lost), was sent immediately to Vienna, while its pendant with flowers and butterflies (ill. 149) remained in Florence. Thanks to the aquatic shades of the background alabaster, these flowers and butterflies, still pulsing with life and colour, seem trapped in the iridescent surface of a frozen pool. This marvel also fascinated Napoleon's French administrators, who after the conquest of Tuscany transferred the tabletop to the Louvre, where it has remained. The replica of the tabletop with shells, which Peter Leopold had copied from the Viennese model for the Palazzo Pitti in the first years of his reign, was also taken to France to become part of the personal furnishings of Josephine Beauharnais at Malmaison.

Peter Leopold of Habsburg-Lorraine succeeded to the Grand Duchy of Tuscany as the younger son of Francis Stephen (Emperor of Austria from 1745) and established his residence at the Palazzo Pitti. With this move the city once more enjoyed a court, and consequently a more brilliant social and artistic life. The director of the manufacture, Cosimo Siriès, who had succeeded his father Louis, was ready to profit from the changes by proposing works to the new Grand Duke for their 'natural' destination, the Palazzo Pitti. Among these were also replicas, produced between 1776 and 1780, of the aforementioned inlays of *The Four Arts*. In these

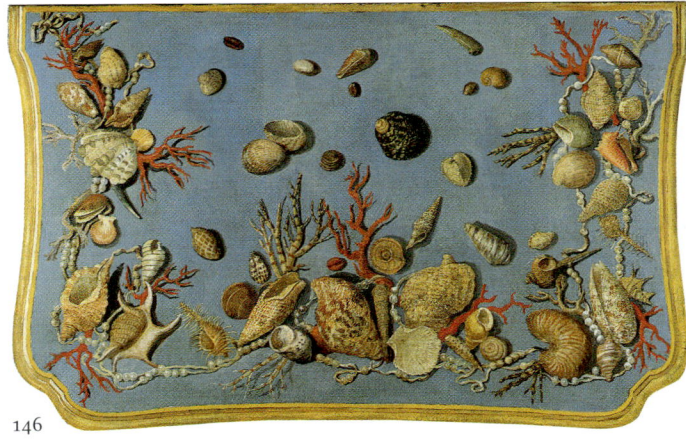

146

replicas, inlay masters well practised in treating the 'figure subjects' of the large Viennese series confirmed their perfect mastery of the equally flexible and arduous naturalness of rendering subjects that seemed to belong exclusively to painting. Yet, the same subjects enjoy autonomy of expression, thanks both to their acute sensibility to the nuances of the marble palette, and the magisterial connection of minute and sinuous sections that vie with the fluidity of brushwork.

The innovative frames of *The Four Arts*, now in the Museo dell'Opificio, are not bronze, as in the Viennese series, but were executed in inlay in the neoclassical guise of *fasces* bound by ribbons. At their corners they include the emblems of the Arts, represented as if they were exquisite passages from a still life. This is one of the first appearances of the new subject matter that would establish itself in inlay during the last twenty years of the eighteenth century, encouraging a classical inclination that fled from any taint of the 'picturesque'. Panoramas and genre scenes continued to be discarded by the third generation of Siriès, Luigi, who had flanked his ageing father Cosimo as director, and who preferred 'ornamental painting, like that which requires fewer shades, and creates more decisive and pronounced borders', as Zobi, the first and best-documented historian of the Opificio, records almost a century later.

146. *Allegory of Water*, model by Giuseppe Zocchi for a console top, 1760. Florence, Museo dell'Opificio delle Pietre Dure

147. Tabletop enlarged in the nineteenth century, but originally a console top after the model by Zocchi (ill. 146). St Petersburg, Hermitage

147

148. *View of a Rustic Interior*, hardstone panel after a model by Antonio Cioci, c. 1772. Paris, private collection

149. Detail of a console table in hardstones with the *Allegory of Air*, after a model by Giuseppe Zocchi, 1765. Paris, Musée du Louvre

The painter Antonio Cioci (d. 1792) decisively embarked in this new direction. In 1771 he took the post in the manufacture that had been left vacant on Zocchi's death. Among the first works based on Cioci's designs was probably the *Assumption of the Virgin* on the *paliotto* of the high altar of the Duomo at Pisa, commissioned in 1773 by Bishop Francesco dei Conti Guidi (Peroni 1995). In his models for inlay panels (ill. 148), Cioci initially seems to have followed the example of his predecessor Zocchi, painting views and genre scenes that were, however, already distinguished by a steady light which fixed the image, giving it a dry appearance, and anticipating the incisive still lifes that would dominate the inlays Cioci would design in the 1780s (González Palacios 1986; Giusti 2002).

New expressive possibilities opened up for hardstone mosaics. Although they risked 'freezing' the mobile and rocaille pictorialism of figure compositions, they were naturally suited to translating Cioci's rarefied compositions of vases or shells into a glossy, frozen splendour. Cioci, in fact, eschewed the domestic still lifes of Tuscan pictorial tradition for hardstone compositions (ill. 150) and preferred courtly subjects with *all'antica* vases, updated in the archaeological mode of neoclassicism, or marine compositions. In the latter the coral, pearls and shells that spread over the surface are not only a pretext for supremely elegant ornament, but also an occasion for a disarming realism that pleased Peter Leopold's Enlightenment court. Not coincidentally, the manufacture registers of the epoch record the arrival of conch shells brought from the Museo della Specola to allow both painters and craftsmen to examine these masterpieces of 'natural art'.

Yet, in inlay the credibility and descriptive fidelity of such subjects, including compositions of Ginori and Japanese porcelain (ill. 151) that can still be recognized in the Palazzo Pitti collections, acquires an abstraction as limpid as it is sublime. This abstraction is only increased by the surreal presence of a stone 'fragment' – like a meteorite descended from the distant stars to become the plane of the composition, illuminated by a steady light that exalts the adamantine quality of the materials. These backgrounds are often of antique red porphyry, a stone whose reputation had never waned and which enjoyed renewed esteem during the neoclassical era. But other stones more recently adopted by the manufacture were also used, like Egyptian nephrite, a stone like dark green velvet and very popular in subsequent nineteenth-century production, where it would be used for 'nocturnal' backgrounds. At the end of the eighteenth century, however, the delicately luminous colours favoured in contemporary applied arts dominated stone inlay: Corsican jasper, light green and iridescent as the sea surrounding the island from which it came; the petrified wood that ranged in hue from dove-grey to pink; opalescent and glacial jade; the dazzling azure of the eternal lapis lazuli.

While this series of new creations left the manufacture to bring a happy close to a century that had threatened the end of the Medici workshops, the effulgent altar that Ferdinando I and his successors had commissioned for the Cappella dei Principi was dismembered and partially dispersed. In the mid-seventeenth century this almost finished, monumental jewel had been assembled within the workshops, where it had remained to become the object of general admiration to those visitors allowed the privilege of seeing it. In 1779 it was dismantled, the mountings in precious metals melted down, the gems that had studded it confiscated, and the hardstone inlays, reliefs and sculptures dispersed or reused on three new altars: in the Villa at Poggio Reale, the Basilica di San Lorenzo and the palatine chapel of the Palazzo Pitti, the last pair still in construction in the eighteenth century.

The Grand Ducal manufacture had to re-elaborate and give free rein to its creative energies, in step with the tastes of the time. This was the inspiring criterion of the director Luigi Siriès, who showed himself more preoccupied than the new Grand Duke with maintaining high artistic levels and rates of production. Thus, in the 1790s, the zealous Siriès proposed making a sort of *Florentiner Zimmer* for the Palazzo Pitti, furnished with inlay panels following the example of the prestigious mid-century project for the imperial residence in Vienna. Although Siriès favoured the now proven, non-figurative subjects for hardstone inlays, he chose fashionable subjects from contemporary painting for the Pitti, such as *Views of Ancient Rome*, a theme that was idolized by neoclassical taste and disseminated by Piranesi's engravings.

Works began but were never finished due to turbulent political events. The series started with six models in oils on canvas by the little known Roman painter Ferdinando Partini, to which figures were added by the more gifted Giovan Battista dell'Era, a personal friend of Siriès (Calbi 2000). Dell'Era inserted exquisitely painted characters as the elegant protagonists of 'conversation pieces' (ill. 152) within Partini's mannered architectural scenes. Four hardstone versions (ill. 153) were made from the models between the last years of the

At the end of the eighteenth century the painter Antonio Cioci introduced still lifes in a neoclassical style into Florentine inlay:

150. Tabletop in porphyry, with a composition of antique vases, 1784. Florence, Galleria Palatina

151. Tabletop with Ginori and Japanese porcelain, executed towards 1792 in the Florence manufacture after a model by Antonio Cioci. Florence, Galleria Palatina

eighteenth century and the first years of the next, by which time the manufacture had come under French control. In 1799, in fact, the Grand Duke had to flee Florence in the face of the Napoleonic advance, and numerous hardstone furnishings were among the artworks stolen from Florence to stock Parisian collections (González Palacios 1986).

However, the period of French domination over Florence also left a less negative mark on Florentine inlay by saving the manufacture from the threat of closure and ensuring that it would continue into the next century – its last, though still an extremely active one in its long and prestigious history. The Napoleonic whirlwind instead wreaked havoc on another royal workshop in hardstones, that in the Buen Retiro at Madrid, which ended its brief but brilliant history in 1808.

This workshop had been founded in 1761 on the initiative of Charles III of Bourbon, the second workshop of the sort that the king had founded when he ruled the Two Sicilies (1738–59). He had lured ten glyptic and inlay specialists to Naples from the Florentine Galleria dei Lavori, then apparently on the verge of extinction along with the Medici dynasty. In 1732 the future King of Naples, who should have inherited the Grand Duchy of Tuscany by descent, spent six months in Florence. There he frequented the Galleria dei Lavori with special interest, the same workshop to which he would turn five years later to enlist Francesco Ghinghi and other artisans to transfer to Naples and activate a similar workshop, abandoning the Tuscany that the European powers had awarded as territorial compensation to the Lorraine family because it had lost its original feud.

The first director of the Naples manufacture, housed in San Carlo alle Mortella, where it would remain active until the advent of the Kingdom of Italy (González Palacios 1979; 1980; 1984), was Francesco Ghinghi, a specialist in cameos and carving, who would leave an account of the first years of the Neapolitan workshop in his aforementioned autobiography (González Palacios 1993). Ghinghi explains to great effect that, because of the loss of the superlative Medici patrons, the artisans at the Galleria were so 'reduced to the final extremes of perdition' that the King of Naples' offer to employ as many artisans 'as would serve for maintaining the Art of both bas-relief and inlay' seemed an unimaginable salvation.

This group of ten Florentine artisans included four specialists in bas-relief, four 'inlay masters', a craftsman entrusted with the initial cutting of the hardstone 'slices', and finally an ebonist. All in all they composed a team capable of recreating, on a reduced scale, the activity of the Florence manufacture that Charles III of Bourbon had witnessed and admired during his youthful sojourn at the court of Gian Gastone de' Medici.

In Naples, complementary but essential posts like that of the 'bronze specialists', who produced the sumptuous mountings that baroque taste loved to couple with hard-

150

stones, and which had been occupied by craftsmen employed directly by the Florence manufacture, were farmed out to specialists, such as the Roman Giacomo Ceci. It was Ceci who, in 1749, made the marvellous gilt bronzes that adorn a couple of small tables now in the Prado (González Palacios 2001). The lively modelling, pervaded by a rocaille spirit, of these bronze cartouches and volutes framing the hardstone tabletops represent the most modern and innovative aspect of this superb pair of tables, begun in 1739 to the designs of the workshop masters. These tables still cling to the late baroque style that inspired Florentine inlay in both the last years of the Medici and the first years of the Habsburg-Lorraines. Indeed, the Prado tables exhibit exactly the same expert choice and display of stones in 'arabesques, fruits, flowers, birds or other delights', as Ghinghi himself tells us.

Perhaps the lack of a sufficient assortment of stone samples in Naples, unlike the collection accumulated so tenaciously by the Medici in Florence, determined the slow progress of work on the two tables. When they were begun in 1739, it was estimated that only two years' work were necessary to complete them, but in the end a whole decade was spent laboriously seeking the right 'marks' in the stones, some of which had to be sent from Florence. Not surprisingly, the Neapolitan court repeatedly criticized the crawling pace of the workshop, and this sluggishness seems to be confirmed by the overall paucity of works, however excellent, that were to issue from it, even though it remained active until 1861.

The most critical years seem to have been those after Charles of Bourbon's departure for Spain in 1759, when it was proposed to close both the hardstone workshop and

the Tapestry works, as we gather from a letter from Luigi Vanvitelli. Vanvitelli laments, 'this new edict will certainly save money...but every decorous light in the Arts will also be extinguished.' He had personal reasons to lament the demise of the workshop at San Carlo alle Mortella: in 1753 it had begun to work on his grandiose design for an altar in hardstones for the chapel in the Royal Palace at Caserta, although countless delays meant that it too remained unfinished.

A second pair of tables in the Prado, also teeming with birds and flowers on a black ground, suffered a long gestation (González Palacios 2001). In 1749, with the first pair of tables already consigned, the second pair were begun, only to arrive in 1763. In this case too, the late baroque inlays of the table-tops are impeccable in design and execution, but particular care was lavished on the fantastic supports in the form of horses' hooves, 'harnessed' with lapis lazuli plaques framed by gilt bronze cartouches, that rise to encircle the tabletop with an unfettered and appealing garland of decorative and sculptural inventions. Among these are the corner heads in high relief portraying *The Four Seasons*, also cast and gilded by Ceci to 'grisaille designs made for the service of the Galleria' by the Florentine Giovanni Morghen, a painter and engraver. Morghen was one of those external collaborators on whom the Naples workshop depended to fill the gap in 'creative' artists that would have been permanent staff members at the Medicean manufacture.

152. *View of the Arch of Janus in Rome*, preparatory model by Ferdinando Partini (landscape) and Giovan Battista dell'Era (figures), 1796–98. Florence, Museo dell'Opificio delle Pietre Dure

153. The hardstone version of the model in ill. 152. Madrid, Palacio Real

155

156

154. Florentine tabletop, with tray of fruit, flowers and birds, from the second half of the eighteenth century. St Petersburg, Hermitage

155. Console top with string of pearls and fan, executed by the Royal Manufacture of Naples, 1773-87. Caserta, Royal Palace

156. Panel with *Small Dog*, from the Florence manufacture. Florence, Museo dell'Opificio delle Pietre Dure

157. Detail of a tabletop with flowers, fruit and birds. Naples manufacture, 1749-63. Madrid, Museo del Prado

Another Florentine, Giovanni Antonio Noferi, otherwise unknown but defined in Neapolitan documents as a 'creator of carvings and excellent inventor of models and designs', collaborated on one of the first works realized by the Naples workshop, a pillar 'for containing Holy Water next to a bed.' This item, executed between 1739 and 1742 (González Palacios 2001), has been lost but it was perhaps inspired by the analogous Florentine artefacts in fashion under Cosimo III. The same holds for the octagonal hardstone plaque with the *Annunciation* and sparkling bronze crown, which was sent from Naples to Madrid and was inspired by the type often replicated in Florence as gifts from the Grand Duke to illustrious recipients (González Palacios 2001).

The referencing of Florentine models began to slacken, without completely disappearing, in the inlays based on models by the Neapolitan Gennaro Cappella (d. 1777), also known as Zampariello, a painter and ornamental artist who had already worked for the Tapestry Works founded by Charles of Bourbon in 1738. Cappella (González Palacios 1979; *Splendori...* 1988) was summoned by the Director, Gaspare Donnini, to work at San Carlo alle Mortella, 'to assist in finding stone markings'. Donnini, an ebonist, had succeeded Ghinghi in the post in 1762 and maintained the position until 1780. Between 1763 and 1768 a couple of wall-panels were executed to Cappella's design. Although they did not renounce the canonical naturalistic themes on a black ground, they did update them with a rocaille verve that widens and animates the wreath of flowers and birds framing the central motif, again a Medicean motif, of a wicker basket and a metal vessel of fruit (ill. 154).

The scheme and palette in a subsequent work based on Cappella's model are not dissimilar, a console top in the Royal

157

Palace at Caserta (ill. 155) whose execution took from 1773 until after 1780. On this console a lively wreath surrounds the traditional *trompe-l'oeil* string of pearls, now modified by the presence of a closed fan that has been apparently left on the table by a distracted lady, forgetful of her genteel accessories. This console was matched by a pendant, perhaps lost in the 1799 sack of the Caserta palace, which replicated a 1781 design by Giovanni Mugnai representing 'in the middle…a small dog that plays with a small bird' (Valeriani 1988). The theme of the small dog, which is very common in rococo painting but rather rare in inlay, does however find a parallel in Florence in a small panel that was never dispatched from the Opificio and which probably dates to the same period (ill. 156).

These and other 'minor' products of the workshop, such as a *schifetta* or serving tray conserved at Kassel (González Palacios 2001), confirm that Neapolitan inlays continued to be based, with cautious thematic and stylistic updates, on the leitmotiv of fruit and flowers on a black ground until the 1780s, by which time such compositions and their intense baroque colouring (ills. 157, 158, 159 & 160) appeared obsolete to emergent neoclassical tastes. The Florentine manufacture had already been moved to experiment with a lighter tonality, new allegorical themes, views and still lifes by the middle of the century. It was followed down this path by the Spanish workshops at the Buen Retiro, established by the same king who had founded those in Naples. There, a new direction only emerged in the 1780s, by which stage Naples had become one of the capitals of neoclassical taste, preferring antique marbles over hardstones, in fact those very marbles in which Vanvitelli (in 1758) found 'nothing rare…in contrast to other hardstones like touchstone, agate, chalcedony…' (Valeriani 1988).

Under the directorship of Giovanni Mugnai, from 1780 to 1805, the workshop was also frequently given to producing tabletops simply veneered with antique marbles, or designed

158, 159 and 160. Further details of the tabletop in ill. 157

to emphasize the intrinsic value of the patterns and colours of the stones. This trend was the inspiration for a superb, circular table (Spinosa 1979) in the Royal Palace at Palermo, recorded in 1795, whose tabletop is almost entirely formed of a great 'slice' of petrified wood, cut from a fossilized trunk that preserved its concentric rings and a colour that ranges from deep brown in the centre to dove-grey shades at the perimeter.

Petrified wood, which had been in vogue in the early days of the Florentine manufacture, now came back into fashion in Naples and Florence in the wake of the interest in the natural sciences sponsored by Enlightenment culture. It was often used for small-format 'gallantries' like frames, fans and particularly tobacco boxes. All of these were industriously produced and enriched with cameos executed by the same Mugnai, a quality carver who had trained in Naples with Ghinghi and who guided the Naples workshops in the trauma-free transition from Bourbon kingdom to French dominion.

We have already noted that the new hardstone workshop founded by Charles of Bourbon in Madrid, shortly after leaving Naples in 1759 to become King of Spain with the name Carlos III, had a much less fortunate fate (González Palacios 1981, 1988, 2001). A true heir of his Medici forebears, as Charles loved to consider himself, in terms of artistic patronage and that special propensity for hardstones, the king installed in the palace of Buen Retiro the porcelain workshop that he had brought with him from Naples. To procure inlay-artists, on the other hand, he turned a second time to Florence and in 1761 managed to recruit Domenico Stecchi, a man who had worked for the 'Imperial and Royal Establishment' of Florence from 1754. This time the Florentine workshops were not caught up in the crisis that had facilitated the earlier diaspora of masters to Naples, but it was still not difficult for the King of Spain to obtain the Grand Duke's permission for Stecchi to leave Florence. The transaction was no doubt expedited by the fact that he was a relative of the Habsburg-Lorraines through the double marriages of Charles of Bourbon's sons with the daughters of Francis Stephen of Lorraine, Emperor of Austria and Grand Duke of Tuscany.

Francesco Poggetti left Florence for Madrid with Stecchi. Poggetti had undergone a long apprenticeship as a hardstone artist in the Ginori workshop at Doccia, where the Ginori had added inlaid tables, boxes and similar furnishings to their already famous and pre-eminent production of porcelain in the mid-eighteenth century. Not much is known about this initiative, probably devised to satisfy the requests of a high-profile and predominantly foreign clientele, which had usually acquired inlays from the Florentine masters who produced them in their free time and at their own expense during the last Medici period, as a contemporary German source recounts (Przyborowski 1998). But the new Habsburg-Lorraine administration had re-established the court monopoly (only interrupted at the century's end) over the output of the hardstone masters. It is therefore likely that the Ginori, who were entrepreneurs in *objets d'art*, were among the first to realize that an independent workshop might capitalize on the fame that Florentine inlays had acquired.

Their example, which seems to have been unique in the eighteenth century, found a much greater following in the nineteenth century when there was a proliferation of inlay workshops producing inlays that closely followed, albeit in more modest forms and materials, the triumphant models of the Grand Ducal manufacture. One can instead deduce from the very few Ginori products known to us today, and sold to clients such as Frederick II of Prussia, that they enjoyed a certain creative freedom. As Sir Horace Mann, an English resident in Florence, noted with chagrin, they also reveal a rather rocaille predilection for white marble grounds with inlays of landscapes or floral shoots that departed from the late baroque style to which Grand Ducal products faithfully clung.

The Madrid workshop at the Buen Retiro was also able to differentiate itself from the Florentine 'mother house', even though its management always remained in the hands of Florentine masters. This was still the case in 1784, by which time the team had grown from the five founder members (Stecchi, Poggetti and son, and two Spaniards) to nineteen, subsequently increasing, under the direction of Francesco's son Luigi Poggetti, to thirty-five workers in 1808, when its brilliant activity was unexpectedly interrupted for good by the Napoleonic wars.

The few decades of the Buen Retiro's short life were nonetheless marked by a modest number of creations, among which a series of nine wall consoles are conspicuous for their originality and allure. They were executed between the late 1760s and 1796, with hardstone tabletops on triumphal supports in gilt bronze, the work of the Italian Giovan Battista Ferroni (González Palacios 2001). The author of the painted models was the Frenchman Charles-Joseph Flippart (1721–97), who had moved to Spain permanently in 1753. There he had been named court painter to Ferdinando VI, and was employed to collaborate with the Tapestry Works and the hardstone workshops, as well as teaching at the Academy (Luna 1981). The tabletops conceived by Flippart, which were magisterial in their execution, fielded *capricci* of ruins populated by contemporary characters, as well as *trompe-l'oeil* of assorted subjects that in some cases frame the central view. Elsewhere, in more coherent and effective inventions, these illusions alone occupy the tabletop on which they seem to have been placed with studied insouciance (ills. 162 & 163).

Although Flippart's views (ill. 161) share some qualities with those recently designed by Zocchi as models for the 'stone gallery' of the Viennese court, it is unnecessary to presume any direct relationship between them. Rather they share a common source, because from 1739 the French painter had frequented the Venetian printing-house of Giuseppe

Wagner, for which Zocchi had also worked. Like Flippart, Zocchi was also attracted to Pietro Longhi's scenes of contemporary life.

To this youthful Venetian inspiration Flippart had then added that of Giovan Battista Tiepolo, who worked for the King of Spain from 1763, and Tiepolo's influence is perceptible in the themes and style of some of the small panels that the Frenchman loved to insert into his *trompe-l'oeil* compositions. In any case, the overall taste of these compositions fits well with the tradition of 'painted deceptions' that enjoyed renewed vigour in contemporary France thanks to the Enlightenment's partiality to detailed and objective images of reality.

Besides such creations, which were the most original and painstaking objects to leave the Buen Retiro, the workshop also dedicated itself to the 'minor' production of tobacco boxes and cameos, genres that were especially in vogue in neoclassical circles, and to large and small panels of views. Conspicuous among the latter for its refinement of execution, perhaps based on a model by Gaspar van Wittel (1653–1736), is the *View of the Grotto of Seiana at Pozzuoli*, a subject that was perhaps particularly pleasing to the nostalgic King of Naples. In the last two decades of the century the workshop also executed a monumental table *surtout*, another genre of 'parade' furnishing that had become fashionable in the neoclassical era and was produced repeatedly, with infinite variations in materials and scenographic composition, until the mid-nineteenth century and beyond. The centrepiece realized at the Buen Retiro, with bronze work designed by Ferroni, and graceful chromatic harmonies of delicate neoclassical quality between pearly alabasters, vivid jaspers and pure amethysts, was given to Napoleon in 1808 by Charles IV of Bourbon to mark their meeting at Bayonne, although the gesture did not save the latter from abdication.

Nor did the precious *surtout* sent to Versailles meet with praise from Napoleonic circles. It was judged to be 'in very bad taste' (Samoyault 1986), and it was soon dismantled and dispersed between various imperial residences. It was also stripped of a good part of its cameos, which were reused to adorn the furnishings of Thomire, as these were more consonant with the majestic display of the Empire. And yet in *ancien régime* France, hardstone inlays had returned to fashion following the reign of the Sun King, when many inlaid furnishings from the royal collections had been sold off and

161. Preparatory model for a console top, painted by Charles-Joseph Flippart for the workshop in hardstones at the Buen Retiro. Madrid, Museo del Prado

162. Detail of a console top from the Buen Retiro workshops, with a view of a port and symbols of the arts, 1779–80. Madrid, Museo del Prado

163. Detail of another console top from the Buen Retiro workshops, with books, silhouettes and small genre paintings, 1781–82. Madrid, Museo del Prado

dispersed, whether Florentine or of the Gobelins manufacture. This happened because a France bewitched by the airy grace of rococo in the first half of the eighteenth century now found the exalted splendour of the materials and the imposing presence of such furniture heavy and outmoded.

At the very most, those furnishings incrusted with the stones dear to the *grand siècle* could now only satisfy growing mineralogical curiosity. Thus some were sent to enrich the natural sciences collection in the Jardin Royal, for which Buffon obtained twelve cabinets from over seventy with stone fittings that were kept in the Louvre. Yet, precisely because of the ambivalence between art and nature that coloured stone inlays purveyed, they returned to fashion in the last quarter of the eighteenth century. Indeed, the Enlightenment's scientific interest in the mineral world contributed to their gradual re-evaluation as artistic creations.

Nonetheless, the brand new objects made in the second half of the eighteenth century were mostly limited to 'learned' selections of stones, often the antique marbles that had returned to vogue with neoclassicism, now enhanced by the grace of the furniture that they adorned. This must have been the case with the 'complete and also rare and precious' collection 'of all the marbles of Italy' that capped the two 'commodes in rose wood, adorned with ormolu', which once belonged to the Marquise de Pompadour (Parker 1964).

The furniture that belonged to Marie Antoinette also frequently included stone inlays, but their preciousness and chromatic qualities contributed to the overall effect without aspiring to become virtually exclusive protagonists in the way that Florentine inlay had dictated. Instead, petrified wood – a geological 'curiosity' that again enjoyed special regard in the eighteenth century – makes up the entire profiled top of the small table that belonged to the same queen. Here inlay is also limited to a twisted ribbon, the elegant pretext for discriminating between the veining of the stone in the central zone and that on the border.

Such circumspection over stone inlays perhaps also resulted from the loss of the technical and working traditions of this difficult art after the closing of the Gobelins workshop. One might suppose this from the degree of industry and fantasy that French cabinetmakers of the neoclassical era or Empire put into employing spare or reused Florentine inlay panels. With as much taste as nonchalance, they often coupled panels that differed in date, subject and provenance, obtaining, however, a sophisticated and elegant ensemble that confirmed eighteenth-century French supremacy in cabinetmaking but did not discard the combination of hardstones, ebony and gilt bronze so popular in the baroque.

One of the most precocious examples of this revival is a cabinet that belonged to the Ducque d'Aumont, a great con-

164. Cabinet by Joseph Baumhauer, c. 1765–70, with gilded bronzes and Florentine inlays. Château de Versailles, Cabinet d'angle du Dauphin

165 and 166. Two of the seventeenth-century inlays used on the cabinet by Joseph Baumhauer

Two examples of French, neoclassical furniture that document the taste for reusing hardstone inlays and reliefs from earlier epochs:

167. *Sécretaire* by Martin Carlin, c. 1780, with seventeenth-century Florentine inlays of landscape and floral themes. Paris, Musée du Louvre

168. Commode by Adam Weisweiler, end of the eighteenth century, with inlays and reliefs from the Gobelins manufacture. London, Buckingham Palace

noisseur of the genre. It was made before 1772, the year in which its creator Joseph Baumauer died. On the front and flanks Baumhauer used twenty-five seventeenth-century, Florentine panels (ill. 164) with the canonical motif of the bunch of flowers and a small bird on a bough of fruit (Davillier 1870). Whether they were taken from dismantled furniture or procured in Florence, which remained well stocked, the fact remains that a few of these panels appeared on the Parisian market in swift response to the new taste. This is confirmed, for example, by the 1772 sales catalogue of Julliot, a section of which is dedicated to 'panels of diverse stones on a black ground', and whose motifs included vases of flowers, birds and fruit. The renewed passion for hardstone inlays also crossed the channel from France, the arbiter of taste, to England where the art dealer Dominique Daguerre opened a shop in 1786 to be nearer the English clientele whose requests had been usually met by his Parisian partner Martin-Eloy Lignereux (Setterwall 1959).

Martin Carlin (active 1776–85) also employed Florentine inlays of the seventeenth and early eighteenth centuries for his furniture, as is evident from the four sunny sea and lake scenes that adorn a *sécretaire* (ill. 167) of around 1780. An even better example is the extraordinary *plein air* 'aviary' – obviously a Florentine masterpiece from the reign of Ferdinando II de' Medici (Giusti 1992) – that forms the tabletop on which Carlin also reutilized old Florentine inlays for the border, with its views and birds on fruit branches.

Another celebrated ebonist who specialized in furniture with hardstone inlays was Adam Weisweiler (1744–1820). His creations often feature both inlay and relief panels manufactured at the Gobelins, in some cases signed on the back by Giachetti and therefore certainly obtained from the dismantled furnishings of Louis XIV. And the hardstones of the Sun King also resumed a place amongst royalty: Gobelins panels adorn two items of furniture by Weisweiler at Buckingham Palace (ill. 168), acquired by the Prince of Wales, the future George IV. Likewise, a magisterial triumph of fruit and flowers in bas-relief, signed by Giachetti, is the central feature of a cabinet in the Weisweiler style, acquired by Charles XIII of Sweden (Setterwall 1959).

Without any real continuity, the fortunes of hardstones and their many creators (such as Weisweiler, who had been successful before the Revolution) passed with the Empire into the new century, where it would experience one last season of success.

CHAPTER 6

From Court Display to Bourgeois Luxury

At the opening of the nineteenth century the political landscape of Europe had been transformed by the expansion of the Napoleonic Empire. Among the many principalities it annexed was also the Grand Duchy of Tuscany, which was now renamed the Kingdom of Etruria and entrusted to Maria Luisa of Bourbon, daughter of Carlos IV of Spain. The regent of Etruria had perhaps inherited from her grandfather, the founder of the Buen Retiro, a lively inclination towards hardstones which her brief Florentine sojourn now gave her the opportunity to demonstrate, by charging the glorious Grand Ducal manufacture with multiple commissions and jealously guarding its monopoly with a *motu proprio* issued in 1806.

This decree (Zobi 1857), in fact, ruled that the 'Establishment' for works in hardstone return to the exclusive service of the sovereign. It was no longer to serve a private clientele, however elite, as had happened during the previous twenty years when the Grand Duke Peter Leopold of Habsburg-Lorraine had granted the artisans this concession, perhaps as part of the austerity cuts that characterized his administration. With this concession the manufacture had ceased to depend entirely on the Grand Ducal finances for its maintenance and could earn funds directly from patrons paying the market price. Even a rapid glance at the registers of the period shows that there was no lack of customers. They are filled with the most illustrious members of the Florentine and Tuscan aristocracy, happy to furnish themselves with precious 'gallantries' in hardstone, whose intrinsic exquisiteness was augmented by the fact that they came from the famous, and for a long time exclusive, Grand Ducal manufacture.

These private sales were, however, on the whole objects of modest format, like jewelry sets (often called 'refinements for a Lady') (ill. 170), tobacco boxes, cases, chivalric decorations, brooches for ball gowns, and so on. They did not take long to make and costs were contained.

The manufacture, which had been used to creating furnishings of royal magnificence for centuries, now began 'democratizing' its courtly products. They were still aimed at a high-ranking clientele, but one that sought out refined objects for personal use rather than the *éclat* of ceremonial furnishings. The preferences of the Napoleonic and imperial regime instead leant in the latter direction, though they were only partially shared by Maria Luisa of Bourbon, who continued to sponsor the manufacture's recent vocation for exquisite trinkets such as jewelry sets, tobacco boxes and monogrammed cases.

169. Large panel with *Vase of Flowers*, executed as a shutter for a cupboard from the Opificio delle Pietre Dure, 1879. Florence, Museo dell'Opificio delle Pietre Dure

170. Necklace with butterflies in hardstones, with gold chain, made in Florence, beginning of the nineteenth century. London, Victoria and Albert Museum

171

172

171 and 172. Watercolour design for the lid of a tobacco box, beginning of the nineteenth century. Florence, Museo dell'Opificio delle Pietre Dure. Tobacco box in hardstones, from the above model. London, Somerset House, Gilbert Collection. This box and the objects on the opposite page are examples of the exquisite quality of Florentine manufacture between the eighteenth and nineteenth centuries.

Yet, alongside these more private delights, there was no lack of representational tables. At least four examples are known to have been made for Maria Luisa, and two of them feature fashionable compositions of antique vases and still lifes of 'produce of the sea'. Indeed, two of the tables in the Spanish royal collections feature shells on a lapis lazuli ground and vases on a nephrite one (González Palacios 2001). These may be compared with a porphyry table with inlays of vases, created between 1800 and 1803, and a circular table with shells, corals and luminously brilliant pearls within a cerulean panel of lapis lazuli, finished by 1807 (Colle 2003).

Both large works like these and more modest ones were executed after the models of Carlo Carlieri. Carlieri did not come from the ranks of professional painters like his predecessors Zocchi and Cioci, but had entered the manufacture as a hardstone worker and had then been promoted to the post of preparing models for inlay. Antonio Cioci, who had happily steered the repertoire of Florentine inlay from figure subjects to rarefied compositions in still life, had died in 1792 and his post had been briefly occupied by his son Leopoldo, to whom only one model can be attributed with any certainty, for an over-elaborate table clock. Carlieri, whose gifts as a subtle and judicious designer cannot have escaped the shrewd director Luigi Sirièes, exclusively produced paper designs, probably because he was not a proficient painter. He was also not particularly original. He was, however, an able disseminator of the neoclassical taste in ornament, which dominates his models in varied assortments. These models often return to the compositions of antique vases and shells that had been produced by Cioci, or feature military trophies, cups of flowers (ill. 171), interlaced torches, lyres, garlands and quivers. This was, in short, the canonical repertoire of contemporary decorative arts, but it loses any trace of cloaked solemnity in Carlieri's designs and instead projects an eighteenth-century taste for genteel elegance, thanks to the light touch of the pen and the soft, watercolour palette.

One of the best examples of Carlieri's talent in ornament is the *surtout*, or centrepiece, that he began for Maria Luisa in 1807 (González Palacios 1986) and completed for the new ruler, Napoleon's sister Elisa Bonaparte, who reigned as Grand Duchess of Tuscany from 1809 to 1815. Elisa also looked upon the celebrated manufacture now under her control with special favour, and among the works that she held dear was the aforementioned centrepiece that had been just started, and which she intended to give to her brother, the Emperor.

The scalloped *plateau*, composed from five pieces, is as sober as it is imperious in elegance, bordered by a palmette frieze in which the golden yellow of the jaspers and the cold opalescence of the chalcedonies stand out luminously against the bluish ground of Persian lapis. This harmony of glacial beauty is repeated in the central zone where two trophies and three garlands lie along the longitudinal axis. For

173. Jewelry set in hardstone inlay, commissioned by Elisa Bonaparte from the Florence manufacture, and mounted in gold in Paris as a gift for her sister Caroline Murat. London, Somerset House, Gilbert Collection *now in Victoria and Albert Museum*

174 and 175. Preparatory model (Florence, Museo dell'Opificio delle Pietre Dure) for the tobacco box with military emblems in gold and hardstones (London, Somerset House, Gilbert Collection). The precious trinkets created by the Florence manufacture in the age of neoclassicism and Empire period were based on watercolour designs, which were subject to modification in execution, as one can see by comparing the model to the lid of this tobacco box.

176. Table with shells and coral on a ground of Corsican jasper, after a model by Carlo Carlieri, c. 1810. Such 'marine creations' entered the repertoire of Florentine inlays in the second half of the eighteenth century and remained popular for a long time. Milan, Museo Poldi Pezzoli

177. Table with antique vases on a nephrite background, 1807. The still life of antique vases recurs in numerous versions in the Florentine inlay between the end of the eighteenth and the early nineteenth centuries. Madrid, Instituto Valencia de Don Juan

the warrior emperor the classical theme of the panoply was especially appropriate, and after its first appearance on the Napoleonic *surtout* it became enduringly rooted in the manufacture's ornamental repertoire (ill. 175), where we find other and more evocative examples. Originally, the celebratory intention of the work that Elisa planned for her brother was meant to have been amplified by a temple, at the centre of the tray, with amethyst columns and inlays of emerald plasma, lapis and other precious stones, enlivened by gilt bronze and silver sculptures and ornaments. These are described in contemporary documents but were never executed. Within the two laurel wreaths was originally also the fateful imperial 'N', which is also documented by a preparatory drawing, but this was erased when Ferdinand III of Habsburg-Lorraine returned to the throne of Tuscany. Ferdinand III obtained the return of the centrepiece, which the princess had carried off in the wake of Napoleon's defeat.

On the other hand, a piece that Elisa commissioned for another of her relatives did reach its destination. This was a rare jewelry set (ill. 173) including a diadem, combs, necklace and bracelet given to her sister Caroline Murat, Queen of Naples, who also had at her disposal the manufacture of hardstones founded by Charles of Bourbon seventy years earlier. Indeed, it has been suggested (González Palacios 1977) that this set, conserved in a leather box with Caroline's royal monogram, was executed for her in Naples. But their refined inlays are incontrovertibly Florentine in subject and style, as a design still preserved in the Opificio confirms, a model for a diadem decorated with shells, pearls and corals. In the final version this model was instead converted into a comb that forms part of the regal set. In the actual montage two 'half-moons' that were turned downwards in the model were inverted to give the item a lively and elegant verve, all decisions that were probably made by the Parisian goldsmiths, whom we know Elisa was used to consulting and who were well aware of their superiority over their Florentine colleagues in this particular field. Indeed, the gold mountings, and particularly the classical and 'Napoleonic' setting of the diadem, are extremely effective. They do not detract from but actually exalt the splendour of the Florentine inlays.

These inlays exhibit the chromatic triad of blue-white-gold that had been employed with equal refinement on the *dessert*, and here they are enlivened by the measured yet dazzling touches of Goan agate used for the corals. Together with the shells and pearls these corals had composed the rarefied 'marine creations' that Cioci had invented thirty years earlier, and which were destined to remain in fashion in both exquisite trinkets and more ambitious works. Among the latter are the numerous tabletops that had adopted the marine theme subject in the eighteenth century, many for private patrons as contemporary registers record, and which would continue to be commissioned by the court during the Empire period. Elisa herself commissioned a table of this kind (González Palacios 1981; Giusti 1992), in which 'marine creations' seem to blossom out of an aquatic background of green jasper from Corsica, and which was ready within a year of her arrival in Florence.

Imperial taste particularly cherished the crystalline green of Corsican jasper and the enamelled luminosity of lapis lazuli, but also the darker and velvety streaking of Egyptian nephrite. The latter made its debut in Cioci's much-loved tables with still lifes of porcelain, and thereafter it was used throughout the entire nineteenth century. Among the works

178. Tabletop finished in 1844 in the Royal Manufacture of Naples, after a model of 1804. Caserta, Royal Palace

from the French period is a small but exquisite table executed in 1807 for Maria Luisa (González Palacios 2001), in which Carlieri arranged with abstract elegance a composition of antique vases (ill. 177), a theme often repeated in his models for both tables and trinkets.

Overall, the French period inaugurated by Maria Luisa and continued under Elisa was stimulating for the manufacture. At first it found itself pressed by demands from the scintillating cosmopolitan society that the Napoleonic wind had blown into Florence, and then, after Maria Luisa's restrictive decree, it was busily employed in royal commissions. In Naples, French control saw Joseph Bonaparte (1806-8) hold the throne, followed by Joachim Murat with his wife Caroline (1808-15). Under their rule the Bourbon manufacture also accelerated its rate of production, which had never been especially intense, and all the more because the first five years of the new century were taken up repairing objects that had been damaged in the sack of 1799. Two exceptions are the semicircular console tables, brand new objects finished in 1804 to the design of the director Giovanni Mugnai (González Palacios 1980), who had assumed the post in 1780 and who died in 1805. These consoles confirmed that taste for 'pictorial' veining that Mugnai had already manifested in the table now in Palermo, a characteristic that was not obscured when the two consoles were joined to make one circular table in 1844 (ill. 178).

The French court's commissions from the manufacture were primarily for tables that formed sample-sets of stones, like the two in the Royal Palace at Caserta with their assorted Sicilian stones, or sober geometric grids of stones enriched by their setting in structures of chiselled elegance. A good example of the latter is the *guéridon* in gilt bronze that was perhaps intended for Napoleon (González Palacios 1981), even though the feminine delicacy of its structure and ornaments hardly seems fitting for the solemn Emperor. This *guéridon* presents a gaming board enclosed by undulating strips of agate, while cameos in coral stud the surrounding band, almost to signal the item's Neapolitan provenance.

We find another evocative variant of the gridded tabletop at Capodimonte, which was begun in the Napoleonic period and supplied with its twin antique Roman *trapezophori* supports in 1835. The tabletop, which is mentioned in a document in 1811 (González Palacios 1981), is an entire transverse section of fossilized tree-trunk, a real geological rarity that would have delighted the natural-scientific interests of an epoch that was the cultural daughter of the Enlightenment. The piece of silicified wood, of notable thickness, that forms the tabletop was cut from a large fragment of fossilized trunk that was later donated along with other materials, when the Naples workshop was closed in 1861, to the Florence Opificio, where it still displays the natural artistry of its veining.

Alongside such works in the 'severe style', the Naples workshops of the Empire period also produced more minute luxuries, like cameos with modern portraits and imitations of antique heads, the speciality of Filippo Rega, or jewelry sets (Spinosa 1979) that included *pettinesse*, the comb-diadems that often crowned the *à l'antique* hairstyles of court ladies. All these works are now mostly known to us from documents, but they sketch a vivid picture of the carving and inlay activities at the workshop in its last brilliant phase. After the Restoration, in fact, the Bourbon sovereigns seem to have lost their family passion for hardstones. Instead, the workshop dedicated itself exclusively to the interminable job of making the ciborium (which was never completed) for the chapel in the Royal Palace at Caserta, and which Vanvitelli had designed back in 1753.

After the Restoration, it was instead from Florence and its still hectic manufacture that a hardstone tour de force reached Naples in 1825 as a gift from the Grand Duke of Tuscany to Francis I, King of the Two Sicilies. This was a circular table of porphyry, with one of the 'usual' but dazzling compositions of shells and corals as its centrepiece (González Palacios 1981).

Such compositions had descended from Antonio Cioci's eighteenth-century inventions into the neoclassical repertoire of Carlo Carlieri; the latter then passed them on to his assistant Giovan Battista Giorgi, who was appointed as official designer to the Grand Ducal workshop in 1815. Even the choice of the material for the ground, ancient red porphyry, still obeyed the neoclassical aesthetic that would dominate the tables made for the Palazzo Pitti in the 1820s. These include a circular tabletop with a vase and trumpet carved in glacial chalcedony that glows against a sanguine ground (ill. 179) (Giusti 1979), and the pair of rectangular tabletops that interweave hunting emblems and musical motifs with indestructible elegance, the overall composition profiting from

179. Detail of a Florentine tabletop with vase, trumpet and olive branch on a porphyry background, 1826. Florence, Palazzo Pitti

the sober harmony of the porphyry ground with the pallid light of the chalcedonies (Giusti 1979).

The choice of porphyry for these and other works in the *ancien régime* style (ill. 180) commissioned by the restored Habsburg-Lorraine dynasty answered not only questions of taste but also economic necessity. The manufacture only had access to off-cuts of this rare archaeological material, which the first Medici Grand Dukes had accumulated in a bundance. The expenditure of the earlier Habsburg-Lorraine administration on the 'Imperial and Royal Establishment for Hardstones' had already been rather contained, but it became even more so after the Restoration, partly thanks to the unimpressive finances of the Grand Duchy of Tuscany. Further signs of thrift come in a pair of tables made around 1819 (Colle 2003), which repeat the still popular compositions of antique vases, but entirely in coloured marbles instead of the hardstones that had always dominated the manufacture and the various versions of the theme elaborated at the time of both the first Habsburg-Lorraines and under the French.

One therefore realizes that homages like the aforementioned table for the King of the Two Sicilies were rare, and in fact the work registers for the years following the Restoration tend to record rather less ambitious works. Articles that recur amongst them with a certain frequency are the 'work boxes' intended for illustrious ladies of the European aristocracy, such as the Princess of Savoy-Carignan, who in 1818 received one that was enriched with gems.

The European fashion for sewing boxes, produced by not only the Florence manufacture but also other workshops, is an index of the growing impact of the bourgeoisie on the aristocracy as the century progressed. But it also manifests a desire for (or even uncontested affirmation of) a feminine model of domestic virtue in open contrast to the provocative nymphs of the Empire style.

180. Tabletop from the Florence manufacture, with emblems from the neoclassical decorative repertoire, 1821. Florence, Palazzo Pitti

In any case, the boxes that the Florentine manufacture produced were endowed with a fragile and feminine grace that foreshadowed that of their future owners. Moreover, the Grand Duke himself took to commenting on the inlay decorations and the stones that were suggested to him by the fourth and last director from the Siriès dynasty, Carlo, who succeeded his father Luigi in 1811. During the period of the last Medici the manufacture had been hard at work, producing small caskets and chests that the Grand Duke could send as gifts. Although these table objects took less time and fewer resources to execute than cabinets, tables or other labour-intensive furnishings, they still spoke the same magniloquent language of baroque court art. Their dimensions were often remarkable, they were liberally adorned on their flanks and lids with hardstone inlays or reliefs and, last but not least, they were always completed with bronzes of imaginative design and refined execution.

An altogether different sobriety marked the post-Restoration caskets meticulously described in the manufacture registers, both in their forms and mountings, which were still dominated by neoclassical moderation in inlays parsimoniously limited to the lid alone. Most have been lost or remain hidden in private collections, and so the whole genre is currently represented by an unpublished example that recently came onto the art market. It's a small rectangular box in gilt bronze with a basalt lid (ill. 181), whose centre is inlaid with three vases resting on a rocky base and four bees at its corners. Both the long and short sides of the box are formed from small slabs of petrified wood with dark central veining. These seem almost to suggest the fantastic profile of mountains against the vibrant and luminous veining of the fossilized wood, a material that had been fashionable in the early days of the manufacture, under Ferdinando I, and had regained its popularity at the end of the eighteenth century.

These little boxes, created fairly frequently in the years 1816–18, are almost always made, like this one, from 'oriental woods', and in some cases the registers record the reuse of elements such as backgrounds or lids from tobacco boxes that had been left incomplete in the manufacture workshops. This may be the case for the slab of greenish basalt with *all'antica* vases and bees, which suit the graceful decorative repertoire of various creations of the designer Carlo Carlieri between the eighteenth and nineteenth centuries. Moreover, his successor Giovan Battista Giorgi, who occupied the same post from 1815, remained faithful to the neoclassical repertoire for at least the first decade of his activity in hardstones, both on tables and small trinkets.

In those years the manufacture also pursued works of greater ambition. The Grand Duke Ferdinand III, in a fit of pride probably prompted by his return to the throne that had been stolen from him by Napoleon, decided finally to complete the Mausoleum in the Cappella dei Medici, which still lacked a vault, pavement and altar. He chose to decorate the dome with frescoes, a decoration that was dignified but far more modest than that planned by its founder Ferdinando I, who had desired an enormous vault, clad with lapis lazuli and gilt bronze rosettes. But for the central altar Ferdinand III returned to the dream of a precious structure in hardstones.

The first model for this altar was designed by the architect Giuseppe Cacialli (1770–1828), who had received the commission to complete the Cappella dei Medici from the Grand Duke in 1818 (Giusti 1979). Various elaborations on the initial idea followed, under the influence of the manufacture director Carlo Siriès. All these projects anticipated the generous reuse of hardstone inlays and reliefs from the preceding epoch that had never been sent away or had returned to the workshops after dismantling. Their reuse would have saved time and money. Nonetheless, some of the inlay panels for the new altar would have to be 'modern', and their design was entrusted to Giorgi, whose work on the scheme until the

181. Sewing chest in petrified wood, with hardstone inlays on the lid, Florence manufacture, second or third decade of the nineteenth century. Private collection

181

182

182 and 183. Panels with liturgical emblems, executed in the Florence manufacture towards 1830–40 after a model by Giovan Battista Giorgi, and utilized in the nineteenth-century assembly of the altar of the Cappella dei Principi. Florence, Cappella dei Principi

183

184 and 185. Detail and overall view of the table of *Apollo and the Muses*, an elaborate creation of the Florence manufacture in the final period of the Grand Duchy of Tuscany, 1837–51. Florence, Galleria Palatina

1840s is documented by models and finished pieces. However, the entire altar was destined never to be assembled, even though plans to do so were still being considered in 1860, as is clear from a drawing of that year by Tito Giorgi, Giovan Battista's son and himself a designer for the manufacture.

In Giorgi's drawing we may recognize four dazzling panels of lapis lazuli with liturgical emblems (Pampaloni Martelli 1979), which had been finished in 1853. The date is confirmed in Zobi's enthusiastic descriptions of the manufacture in his book, which came out in the same year. The oil-on-canvas models that Giorgi prepared for them date from the 1830s and demonstrate the development of his style from neoclassicism (which remains the basis of the design) to a certain ornamental exuberance that infuses both the overall design and the individual forms. As always, the inlay artists were able to indulge and interpret the painted model, translating it into the golden luminosity of the chalcedonies of the liturgical objects and the shadowed chiaroscuro of the bunches of grapes, which forecast Florentine inlay's return to naturalistic subjects in the middle of the century.

A markedly mature expression of this taste is visible in the oval plaquette that was sent to the Princess of Teano in 1829 to decorate the lid of an ebony work box, which has recently resurfaced in a private collection (Colle 2003). The design of the lapis oval is based on a watercolour by Giorgi (which survives to this day) and features a dense bunch of flowers, which are described with a botanical fidelity that recalls seventeenth-century still lifes but, at the same time, rejoices in a vegetal luxuriance that is fully nineteenth-century. For the first time the magnolia, picked out of the bunch by the pearly brilliance of chalcedony, entered the well-stocked floral repertoire of the Florentine manufacture and it was destined to become the trademark of the last products of the second half of the century.

More diffuse evidence of the re-emerging propensity towards natural subjects comes in the masterpiece that absorbed the manufacture's energies in the last years of the Grand Duchy of Tuscany. This is the vast circular table of *Apollo and the Muses*, finished in 1851 but begun in 1837 (Giusti 1979) and equipped with a grandiose figural support in bronze by the sculptor Giovanni Dupré (1817–82) in 1853. The idea for this project came from the director Carlo Siriès, who had seen the court commissions continue to dwindle with the accession of the new Grand Duke Leopold III in 1824. Leopold III often requested tabletops that were simply veneered with the abundant stones in the manufacture stores. This vast table was instead planned to be exemplary and memorable, capable of rivalling any masterpiece of the past, with a complex scheme designed to accentuate its palette of rare materials and virtuosity of execution. Every

227

From Court Display to Bourgeois Luxury

186. Tabletop with garland of roses and shells, Florence manufacture, 1850–60. Florence, Museo dell'Opificio delle Pietre Dure

possible care was therefore taken for the work to satisfy its ambitious expectations. It was decided that the table should be of exceptional scale, only inferior in size to its famous precursor in the Uffizi Tribuna (ill. 72). Likewise, an oriental lapis of a dazzling azure was chosen for the background and a more vivid and varied selection of jaspers and chalcedonies for the ornaments (Giusti 1978).

Giorgi, who was called upon to design the model for this demanding composition, abandoned the works of more contained elegance that had marked his neoclassical origins and devised a complex allegorical and didactic assembly, more in sympathy with trends in the decorative arts in the second quarter of the nineteenth century. The theme illustrated is the triumph of the Arts, represented through the blazing chariot of Apollo at the centre, surrounded by the emblems of the nine Muses. These emblems are incorporated into vegetal borders that combine monochrome chill and neoclassical style with flowering shoots pulsing with life and enlivened by an intense floral palette. Although the inlay artists received bonuses for the overtime required to complete the table, it is easy to understand how it still took fourteen long years to complete given the range of inlays and the immeasurable care and time necessary to find the right nuances in the stones. Indeed, even the lapis lazuli was chosen and laid to emphasize the dark veins, here and there powdered with golden pyrites, which depart from the table's centre giving the impression that the god's chariot is moving within a celestial halo.

Even though this regal table, which would crown the final years of the Grand Duchy of Tuscany, consumed a good part of the manufacture's energies, in the 1840s its indefatigable director Siriès was busy preparing other tables for court, to Giorgi's designs. These last creations from the Habsburg-Lorraine period may have been smaller but they were not without charm. In a rectangular tabletop, porphyry back-

187. Florentine table of 1852, which utilizes foliate panels of seventeenth-century manufacture. Florence, Galleria Palatina

grounds the central 'trophy', and a curling and coloured garland that adjoins, or overlays, the chaste monochromy of neoclassical emblems offers further confirmation of the naturalistic revival displayed in the table of *Apollo and the Muses*.

The eclectic taste that affirmed itself at mid-century also salvaged eighteenth-century ornamental motifs like Cioci's shells, corals and pearls. They appear on a circular table made between 1850 and 1860 (ill. 186). Its dark green veining of Egyptian nephrite ground is as shifting as velvet; a garland of white roses in delicate tones palpitates against it, almost ready to bud, as if kissed by the breath of a waning romanticism.

Alongside works such as these, which displayed the manufacture's creative abilities at their best, it became common practice to reuse Medici-era pieces from the stores in new compositions. This was not just a question of economy but also satisfied the eclecticism and inclination towards pastiche that had become a major trend during the nineteenth century. This taste is all too evident in a table sent to the Palazzo Pitti in 1852 (ill. 187), with a black background and 'antique ornaments at the four corners and in the centre', referring to the panels of lively late baroque foliage contained in slim borders.

On the other hand, this taste for reusing seventeenth-century inlays and reliefs does not appear in Florence before the second quarter of the nineteenth century, whereas in France, which always anticipated trends in European taste, it

had already begun by the end of the eighteenth century. At that time, the most accredited Parisian cabinetmakers had begun to adorn their neoclassical furnishings with hardstone panels that originated in either the defunct workshop at the Gobelins or the abundant Florentine production of the last Medici. The practice never died out. Indeed, it found even more diffuse application as the nineteenth century progressed and the passion for salvaging and blending past styles grew stronger. During the Empire, the cabinets by the ebonist Adam Weisweiler, who had been fortunate enough to retain his celebrity during the passage from the *ancien régime* to the Napoleonic era, had become increasingly massive and dense with gilded bronzes. Weisweiler had also continued to apply Florentine inlays to them, nonchalantly coupling landscape scenes with naturalistic panels of flowers and birds or individual animals mounted in slabs of *pietra albarese dell'Arno*.

England had also been traditionally interested in Florentine inlays, which were *de rigueur* acquisitions for British gentlemen on the Grand Tour, and in the first decades of the nineteenth century Florentine inlays from the preceding centuries were used to decorate furnishings by the major designers of the day. Thus seventeenth-century inlays with naturalistic themes can be found mounted on an imposing cabinet designed by Robert Adam (ill. 188). Six relief panels in hardstones, which are inserted into a table clock and cabinet (ill. 189) executed in 1824 for the Duke of Hamilton to the designs of Robert Hume (active 1804–40), are instead recognizable as rare surviving works from the Gobelins of Louis XIV. The four panels with birds and the pair with garlands and cups of fruit may be compared with others from the seventeenth-century French workshop, while the beautiful floral frieze bordering the clock face, also in relief, was probably commissioned in Florence in order to complete the decorations of this nineteenth-century furnishing (Massinelli 2000).

In England and especially France, in the second half of the century, the 'pompous' taste of the Second Empire, which programmatically affirmed the continuity between the Napoleons, continued to produce furniture so imposing that it was almost oppressive. These furnishings enlivened the slightly funereal harmony of black painted wood with gilded bronze by inserting vivacious panels of Florentine inlays dating from the seventeenth and eighteenth centuries.

A small fireplace, formerly in the collection of Prince Demidoff, is also French. It is clad in malachite; the vibrantly streaked green stone that emerged from the Siberian wastes at the time of Catherine the Great. Malachite had immediately become popular in both Russian and European furnishings thanks to the mediation of France, which made great use of it in the furniture by Thomire and other great artisans of the Napoleonic period. In the hall of the Villa Demidoff at San Donato, in the environs of Florence, among furnishings of regal splendour towered an enormous vase of malachite, made again by Thomire but in the triumphally monumental style typical of the Hermitage in St Petersburg. The Demidoff fireplace, now in the Museo Stibbert, is a little later, and among the bronzes of its architrave and plinth are Florentine panels of baroque taste, with hardstone reliefs of flowery shoots and fruits on a black ground. Prince Anatoly Demidoff (1812–70), whose presence in Florence and 1840 marriage to Mathilde Bonaparte, Jérôme's daughter, cast an aristocratic and cosmopolitan glow on a court that had started to become provincial, received five ovals with flowers and fruits as a wedding gift from the Grand Duke. They bear fascinating testimony to the recent 'reconversion' of Florentine inlay to naturalistic themes, and Prince Anatoly Demidoff had them mounted on a small fireplace of white marble with gilt bronze trim (ill. 193) (Giusti 1992).

The return of the manufacture to floral and naturalist subjects, which Giorgi had inaugurated in his works during the 1830s, achieved its apotheosis in a circular table with birds, flowers and fruit (ill. 194) designed by Giorgi's successor as artistic director, Niccolò Betti. This table was finished in 1855

188. Cabinet designed by Robert Adam in the early nineteenth century, with reused Florentine inlays of the seventeenth century. London, Victoria and Albert Museum

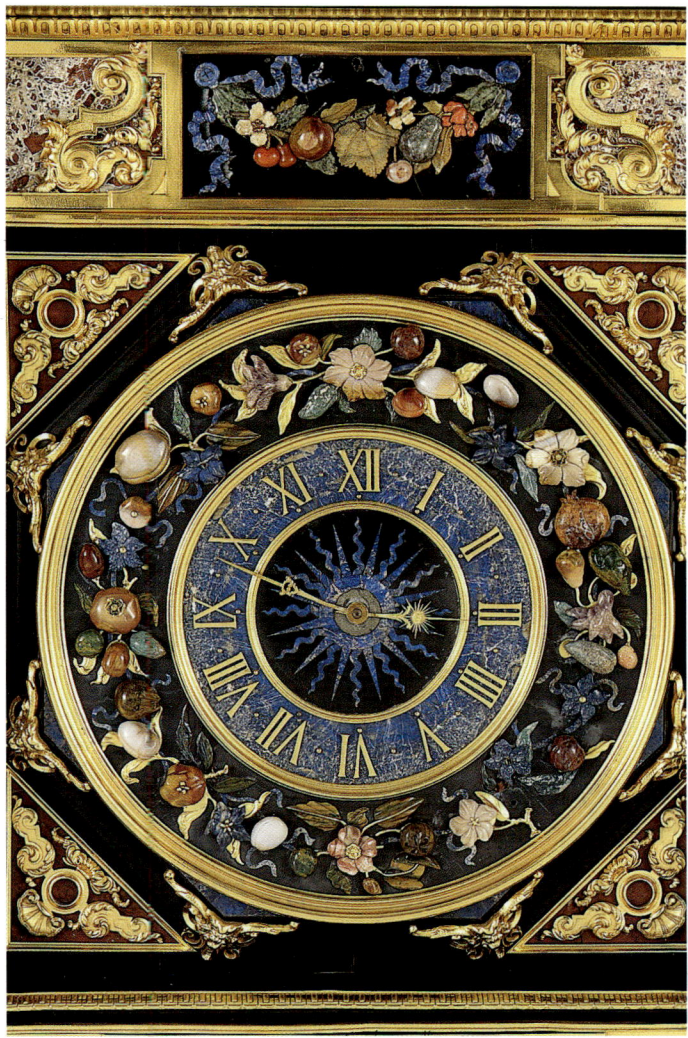

189. Detail of a table cabinet with a clock, designed in 1824 by Robert Hume. The hardstone reliefs date from the seventeenth century. London, Somerset House, Gilbert Collection [now in Victoria-Albert Museum]

and was the last work to arrive at the Palazzo Pitti, which the Grand Duke would leave for definitive exile four years later. Fittingly, then, it seems almost as if the old Medicean manufacture wished to distil its long and glorious history in this work. The undulating and leafy shoots that form two concentric garlands are in the late baroque taste of Cosimo III de' Medici, while the shells that open along the perimeter date back even further, to the highly celebrated table in the Uffizi Tribuna that had been prepared for the wedding of Ferdinando II de' Medici and Vittoria della Rovere. The loving observation of nature that the painter Jacopo Ligozzi had introduced into Florentine inlay in the early 1600s, also returns in the bunches of flowers and fruit that bloom among the baroque shoots and throng the central garland. They are no longer the rare and exotic flowers of sophisticated Medicean botanical collections, however, but the 'domestic' nature of nineteenth-century gardens: roses, jasmine, geraniums and camellias. To represent their hues, as well as those of the small birds posed naturalistically on the stems, the manufacture employed almost the entire, variegated palette of hardstones still available from its old stockpiles, and they pose a radiant and strident foil to the moiré background of Egyptian nephrite.

The manufacture and the Grand Duchy of Tuscany continued to live as though they had no inkling of their imminent demise: in 1857 Leopold II received Pope Pius IX at the Palazzo Pitti and gave him a late eighteenth-century hardstone panel, a *View of the Tomb of Cecilia Metella*, immediately ordering the workshop to replace it with an exact copy. This panel was barely begun in 1859 when the Grand Duke left Florence for the last time, but work continued into the early years of the Kingdom of Italy (unified in 1861), and it would be exhibited at the 1867 Exposition in London (Giusti 1978; Massinelli 2000).

It seems that the manufacture had no conception that the court no longer existed, nor its reassuring rhythms of patronage, which had guaranteed the workshop's artistic vitality for almost three centuries. And yet crucial signs of the changed politics and social mechanisms of the new Italy had come with the closing of the Bourbon workshop at San Carlo alle Mortella in Naples, immediately after the proclamation of a unified Italy, and its stocks of stones were on this occasion transferred to the manufacture in Florence.

The weight of the manufacture's history was such that no decision was taken to close it, even though the Ministry of Public Instruction, on which it now depended, threatened as much several times at the close of the century. Instead the manufacture was transformed into an artistic-commercial organization capable of financing itself by selling its products on the open market. The workshop, which had once been the Medici Galleria dei Lavori, was now renamed the Opificio delle Pietre Dure in homage to a nascent industrial society.

For more than twenty-five years its fortunes were hostage to a conflict between two parties. On the one hand, there were those within the Florentine institute who saw the need to maintain the exemplary artistic standards that had guaranteed its fame for centuries; on the other, external observers,

and foremost the Ministry in Rome, emphasized economic viability and therefore wanted the Opificio to become competitive with the numerous private workshops that specialized in stone inlays in Florence.

Even in the Medici era, private activity had prospered in the shadow of the exclusive court manufacture, more or less with the consent of the Grand Dukes. Indeed, private works were often produced by the Grand Ducal artisans moonlighting on their employ at the Galleria dei Lavori. The independent workshops produced works of good quality, derived from the manufacture models, but mainly panels of modest dimensions that the mostly foreign clients would have mounted on furnishings of their own taste, once home. Among the many examples that fit this bill, but which are not easily distinguished from the rest of the vast Florentine output, are nineteen marble-inlay plaquettes of those naturalistic themes so typical of the manufacture, which John Evelyn acquired in Florence in 1644 from Domenico Benotti. Evelyn himself described Benotti in his diary as 'a celebrated master...in stone inlay.' In this case Evelyn also had the table-cabinet made in Florence, on which the nineteen panels were mounted, which is now in the Victoria and Albert Museum (Riccardi Cubit 1993).

But it was above all the nineteenth century that saw a flowering of private workshops producing Florentine inlays in the city, designed to satisfy the tastes and needs of the new bourgeois clientele. This clientele could not afford the hardstone displays that had dazzled the courtly world of the *ancien régime* but was rather fascinated by the trinkets, tabletop objects, jewelry and other furnishings of 'middling' luxury on which various Florentine inlay workers now focused. Opificio models inspired and ennobled these works, which were often of a high quality from a technical point of view, but whose costs limited them to a reduced range of stones that were mostly calcareous, and therefore easily procured and not hard to work. The fame of these workshops among the international public was also boosted by their participation in the European (though not American) universal exhibitions that were periodically held during the second half of the nineteenth century.

Although recent research has plumbed this field between art and production (Chirarugi 1994; Massinelli 2000; Colle 2001), an exhaustive survey of the artisanal workshops active in inlay in Florence in this period is yet to be achieved. Above all, it is necessary to reconstruct the extent of their production, a hard task given the wide diffusion of the products and the close resemblance of their subjects and technical execution. In fact, private sector artisans were not interested in attempting original creations and studying colour schemes in stone, as the Opificio had always done and continued to do. Instead, they aimed at satisfying the ultimately traditional tastes of a bourgeois public with products of proven success, such as the still lifes and floral compositions that were varied and pleasing versions of the Opificio prototypes.

Amongst the most famous and active of these workshops was that of Gaetano Bianchini. In 1825 Bianchini put his youthful apprenticeship at the manufacture in the Grand Ducal era to good use by opening his own workshop, which remained active under his heirs until the end of the century. The activity of a certain Francesco Betti is also documented for the years 1848-84, though his production remains to be identified, and the Buoninsegni brothers were active in the

190 and 191. Detail and overall view of a commode in the Second Empire style. The inlays with landscapes and figures are of Florentine manufacture from the seventeenth and eighteenth centuries. St Petersburg, Hermitage

middle years of the century when they presented their creations at great exhibitions in London (1851) and Paris (1855).

On the other hand, there is no other record of the Scappini, who signed a hardstone tabletop at Somerset House (ill. 197) (Massinelli 2000). This displays a still life inlaid in the classic black ground of Belgian marble. Rather unusually, it also features a large pumpkin that rests, along with the rest of the composition, on a support in the form of a stone 'fragment', a motif often present in works from the second half of the century and derived from the designs that the painter Antonio Cioci had invented a century earlier at the Grand Ducal manufacture. Another of Cioci's highly effective inventions had been still lifes with vases. While these seem to have been of marginal interest to the Opificio – in spite of its tendency to salvage old models in the last years of its activity – they recur with a certain frequency in inlays produced by private Florentine workshops. These workshops often added evocative accessories like corals, shells, pearls and ribbons to neoclassically inspired still lifes with *all'antica* vases (ill. 196), accessories that Cioci had used to enliven his own inanimate compositions. Occasionally the workshops also chose red and quintessentially classical porphyry for the background of these compositions, rather than the more common and less costly black marble of Belgium. This is true for a beautiful tabletop (ill. 198) from the late nineteenth century still preserved in Florence in the Ugolini collection (Massinelli 2000), one of the most able family workshops at the century's end and one that kept abreast of the latest creations at the Opificio, as the great magnolia flowering from the central crater attests. The magnolia became a trademark of the Opificio in the 1870s and 1880s.

The workshop founded by Enrico Bosi in 1858 may be considered a sort of private Opificio for two reasons: first, the quantity of craftsmen employed, which reached the remarkable number of thirty-six in the 1860s; secondly, the favour that it met among a vast clientele, which it accessed through the Universal Expositions and salesrooms in Turin, London and Paris. The furnishings of the Bosi firm, which included ebonists and bronze workers, also met with the approval of Victor Emmanuel II of Savoy (1820–78), who showed no great interest in the manufacture that had been dear to the Grand Dukes during his own stay in Florence. In 1861, at the Italian Exposition in Florence, the King acquired from Bosi a monumental cabinet for the Palazzo Pitti, where it remains (Colle 2001). Among the palace furnishings there also survives a graceful toilette ensemble, trimmed with the bronzes and lapis lazuli – a characteristic of Bosi's productions (*Curiosità*... 1979).

But the Opificio did receive one court commission, a table that was sent to Costantino Nigra (1828–1907), minister of the Royal House, in 1863 (Pampaloni Martelli 1978). This work remains untraceable for the moment, but because of its octagonal form and composition of flowered panels along the sides and a bunch of flowers in the centre, we may suppose that it was the first version of another table made in 1878 (ill. 201), this time with fruit decorations rather than flowers. Another creation destined for the Court of Savoy was an exquisite casket, this time commissioned by the Ministry of Public Instruction as a gift for the 1868 wedding of Margaret of Savoy with the hereditary prince Humbert (Norcini 2004). This object, which enclosed an autograph doc-

192. Detail of a table with central motif of doves, and small birds on the border, 1870. Florence, Museo dell'Opificio delle Pietre Dure

193. One of five chimney plaques sent as gifts from the Grand Duke Ferdinand III of Habsburg-Lorraine to Prince Anatoly Demidoff, *c*. 1840. Florence, Museo Stibbert

194

ument of Alessandro Manzoni, had a structure in ebony and gilt bronzes in the historicist taste of the epoch and on the lid a hardstone inlay of bunched flowers. In fact, flowers, an old passion of the Florence manufacture, once more became a guiding theme in the production of the second half of the century, alongside occasional products inspired by eighteenth-century models. The latter products included the aforementioned tabletop of a *guéridon* with vases, now more neoclassical than antique in form, and a *Resting Shepherds*, which was finished in 1879 but would not have been out of place among the rural scenes painted by Zocchi and Cioci (Giusti 1978).

Another member of the House of Savoy, Maria Pia, Victor Emmanuel II's daughter and Queen of Portugal from 1862, included some Florentine inlays among her furnishings at the Palacio da Ajuda, Lisbon. In this case they came from private workshops, like the monumental cabinet in wood, bronze and hardstones (ill. 203), inspired by models from the first half of the seventeenth century and signed by a certain 'Luigi Resi, living in Florence at Piazza dei Pitti No. 17' (*Tesauros Reais* 1992). One cabinet and a circular table also follow the Opificio models so closely that they could be confused with its output, were it not for the lesser expertise in the choice of the stone palette. The façade of the table-cabinet displays neo-Renaissance panels with shoots of domestic flowers based on those that the Opificio produced in the 1860s and 1870s, while the circular table is bordered by a dense festoon of flowers containing a composition of grapes and vine leaves.

The naturalistic theme of fruit and vine leaves had rarely been exploited in the old repertoire of inlay, even though Florentine panels had systematically explored the natural

194. Detail of a table with flowers and birds, of 1855, the manufacture's last important work for the Grand Duke of Tuscany. Florence, Museo dell'Opificio delle Pietre Dure

195. *View of the Tomb of Cecilia Metella*, made in the Florence manufacture in 1860 after a late eighteenth-century model. Florence, Museo dell'Opificio delle Pietre Dure

196. *Guéridon* with vases in neo-Renaissance style, made at the Opificio, 1870–80. Florence, Museo dell'Opificio delle Pietre Dure

197. Detail of a tabletop with a *Still Life*, from the second half of the nineteenth century, signed 'F. Scappini, Florence' and inspired by contemporary works executed by the Opificio delle Pietre Dure. London, Somerset House, Gilbert Collection

world. However, it now became one of the favourite subjects of Niccolò Betti, director of the manufacture from the last days of the Grand Duchy until 1876. It was Betti's decision to 'reconvert' the Opificio inlays back to naturalistic themes, a shift already begun under Giovan Battista Giorgi. Betti, however, brought the 'conversion' to a head and then passed it on to his successor Edoardo Marchionni.

A document of 1863 speaks of a table with only grape decorations (ill. 199). Two years later a circular tabletop still preserved at the Opificio followed suit. The success of this object hangs on the modulated and sophisticated, almost monochrome, harmonies between Sicilian jaspers for the vegetal parts and dewy chalcedonies for the grapes themselves (Pampaloni Martelli 1978). This inlay is so sophisticated that the modern visitor to the Museo dell'Opificio may recall Pliny's famous anecdote on the realism of a painting by Apelles and imagine that, when the museum lights are out, the small birds take flight from the neighbouring *Table with Doves* (ill. 192) and peck at the chalcedony grapes.

The predominance of naturalistic themes that Betti imposed on the manufacture continued under his successor, Edoardo Marchionni, who took the reins in 1876. Marchionni

was a painter of moderate talent who had trained at the nearby Accademia and entered the Opificio in 1868 (Pampaloni Martelli 1976). His rapid rise through the ranks was due not just to undoubted artistic ability, but probably also to 'managerial skills', as we would call them today. These skills led him first to fight strenuously for maintaining the high prestige of Opificio products, which met with the incomprehension and obstruction of the Ministry, and then to take realistic stock of the changed conditions. As a result, he guided the transformation of the Opificio from being a courtly survivor from a vanishing world to a 'functional' laboratory for restoring works in stone, and one that was highly sought after in the new activity of maintaining the artistic patrimony of the State.

Yet, before this metamorphosis, which has had lasting effects on the vitality and make-up of the present Opificio (Acidini Luchinat 2001), artistic production under Marchionni was distinguished by quality and ambition as it scrambled to bring itself up to date with the most current trends in European decorative arts. As Betti's collaborator in his final and ailing years, Marchionni had already succeeded in directing certain works towards a high-quality clientele on a par with the patrons of the past. In 1870 the Tsar of Russia acquired a version of the *Apollo and the Muses* table that had been sent to the Palazzo Pitti twenty years earlier. The Tsar's version, redesigned by Marchionni, was smaller in size and on a black ground, however. In 1875 a tabletop was also sent to one of the fairy-tale palaces of Ludwig II of Bavaria (González Palacios 1981, II), which attempted the unusual coupling of tessera mosaic, in the great heraldic centrepiece, with hardstone inlay.

In 1870 a panel of the *Christ Praying in the Garden of Gethsemane* (ill. 202) reached another premier destination when it was sent as a gift from the Florentine Curia to Pope Leo XIII (González Palacios 1981, II). This work allowed the artisan Paolo Ricci to show off the best of his glyptic abilities. In the 1850s, in fact, Betti had steered the manufacture back to the tradition of sculptural carving in hardstones, which had been abandoned at the time of Cosimo III but now satisfied a late nineteenth-century historicism determined to reclaim past styles and forms. The final flowering of hardstone sculpture at the Opificio in the late nineteenth century in fact saw Ricci as its main protagonist, an artist that had entered as an apprentice in 1855 and remained active until his death in 1892. Ricci was inspired less by the baroque exuberance of the virtuoso carver Giuseppe Antonio Torricelli than the more contained statuettes of *Evangelists* from the first half of the seventeenth century. Ricci tried his hand at both relief and sculpture, with subjects derived in the latter case from the historic and 'patriotic' repertoire fashionable in contemporary statuary like the exquisite *Cimabue* sent to the Vienna Exposition of 1874 (Pampaloni Martelli 1978), whose finely crafted robes are incongruously but pleasingly inspired by the Trecento dandies frescoed in the Cappellone degli Spagnoli.

But Ricci was also capable of adapting his flexible talent as a carver to other subjects, like the masks of Chinese inspiration in red Cypriot jasper that pay homage to the fin-de-siècle orientalist trend by decorating the projections of a monumental flower-stand of 1883. This was made to the design of Marchionni, who even in these final works of the Opificio sought to flaunt creations equal to the past magnificence of the manufacture. Offered for sale at the exorbitant price of 65,000 lire (Pampaloni Martinelli 1978), the flower-stand remained unsold, even though it boasted a crowning of exquisite inlays designed by Marchionni, which prefigure the tendency in post-Macchaioli Tuscan painting towards the more up-to-date art nouveau. This tendency is perceptible in both the airy embroidery of flowers, much like that of a Japanese screen, and in the 'Botticellian' *Flora*, reinterpreted in the carnal hedonism of the Belle Epoque (ills. 205 & 206). Though the Opificio was normally imitated by private Florentine workshops, this rare and excellent move into figurative subjects seems to have had no following. Yet the late nineteenth-century public showed that it enjoyed Florentine inlay. It preferred, however, the kind that imitated contemporary painting, in which the Montelatici workshop specialized. This workshop had been founded by Giovanni Montelatici in the 1890s and continued under his sons Alfonso and Mario. Perhaps designs of some originality resulted from the Montelatici collaboration with Galileo Chini, who designed the model for a table, now lost, with an *Annunciation* displayed at the 1900 Paris Exhibition. On the whole, although the Montelatici workshop's prolific production of figurative subjects were well executed in terms of choosing the best stones to render the vibrant touches of contemporary pictorial style, in reality they made Florentine inlay into an artistically expressive 'servant', a mere imitation of painting.

This type of work was well adapted to the tastes and wallets of fin-de-siècle clientele, with whom Marchionni did not wish to compromise in his proud defence of the artistry and personality of the glorious Opificio tradition. This tradition was reaffirmed one last time in another great creation: a monumental vase of touchstone (Pampaloni Martelli), second only in size to the giants of Tsarist manufacture but unique for its decoration. The vase's coupled inlay – much more difficult to cut because it had to follow the convex surface – has a high relief that almost blooms from the vital tangle of vegetation and animals, which constrain the sensual form of the vase and spread over it. Work began on the vase in 1882, and in 1891 it was left unfinished because of the Opificio's new commitments to art restoration, undertaken by Marchionni so as not to fatigue or unnecessarily waste the prestigious technical expertise of the manufacture's artisans in minor works.

It was a wise choice, one that would guarantee the old Medicean establishment a vital presence, although one can only mourn the splendours of times past – glories that are reborn every time the stones of the past recuperate some of their lost life in the hands of today's restorers. It is as though the Medici live again, the old patrons of these marvels, when the workshop they created revives a lifeless table from the time of Ferdinando I, or the mausoleum of polychrome marbles that Cosimo III sent to Goa for the tomb of St Francis Xavier (ills. 57 & 204). Cosimo's motto, *Certa fulgent sidera*, belied a reign that would end shortly, but it may instead hold true for the history of the 'family' manufacture. The impetus that they gave it has not yet ended, and the hardstones still sparkle.

198. Tabletop in porphyry, executed at the end of the nineteenth century by the Ugolini workshop in Florence. Private collection

199. Tabletop with grapes and vine leaves, executed by the Opificio after the model of Niccolò Betti, 1865. Florence, Museo dell'Opificio delle Pietre Dure

200. Tabletop with garland of flowers and bunches of grapes, Florentine workshop of the second half of the nineteenth century. Lisbon, Palacio da Ajuda

201. Octagonal table with cup and branches of fruit, executed by the Opificio in 1878. Florence, Museo dell'Opificio delle Pietre Dure

202. *Christ Praying in the Garden of Gethsemane*, relief inlay made at the Opificio by Paolo Ricci, 1870. Rome, Vatican Museums

203. Table cabinet with bronzes and hardstone inlays. Lisbon, Palacio da Ajuda

204. Table with polychrome inlays on a white ground. Madrid, Museo del Prado

205 and 206. Two crowning panels from a monumental flower stand, in marble and hardstones. Among the works that concluded the long activity of the Florentine manufacture, it was finished in 1883 to the design of Edoardo Marchionni. Florence, Museo dell'Opificio delle Pietre Dure

CHAPTER 7

How a Florentine Mosaic is Born

The complex sequence of tasks that culminates in the realization of a Florentine mosaic, and which was perfected in the sixteenth century, has remained substantially unchanged over the centuries in the workshop founded by the Medici and the court workshops it gave rise to. The sequence remains complex, although the artisanal tradition that developed alongside or in the wake of superb prototypes also disclosed it in more simplified forms. The imitations can be recognized in the (not always ideal) manner in which pre-existing models are adapted for new purposes, in the choice of relatively complex images, and in the prevailing adoption of a restricted and economic range of 'soft' coloured stones (stones of calcareous nature). In any case, what unites the noble Grand Ducal examples with the products of artisanal workshops, whose activity continues in Florence to this day, is their completely manual production, using only traditional tools, and the various stages of execution entailed in order to make the final product.

We will, therefore, examine these different phases, just as they were carried out within the Florentine manufacture, the 'mother' and model for all other 'branch' workshops in the genre. The basis for each Grand Ducal intarsia was an original painting, a 1:1 model, specially commissioned from an artist for this purpose. As early as the sixteenth century and continuing over the following centuries, the model could be painted in oils on canvas, like a true painting, or more often in watercolour on paper (ill. 207). The colour scheme of the model had to take into account the natural 'palette' offered by the stones, without being unduly constrained by them. The eventual object of admiration was, in fact, not a mere translation of the original image from one technique into another but a free transposition, made possible by the vast palette of stones at the craftsmen's disposal and by their imaginative interpretation of the colours suggested by the model.

This task was entrusted to the master responsible for the inlay, whose execution was normally subdivided amongst several craftsmen in order to reduce the working time, which remained quite long for objects of large dimensions. For example, it took eighteen craftsmen eleven years to complete the table in the Tribuna of the Uffizi. The master took a tracing from the model in pen or pencil, on which he marked the stone sections to be assembled into the entire image (ill. 207). This initial 'breakdown' of the model was a delicate phase because the number and profile of the sections would have a decisive impact on the final quality of the executed inlay. Still more decisive and laborious was the subsequent stage, which involved selecting the right stones for the job. The utmost patience and judgment were necessary in order to choose

207. Model, watercolour on paper, and the tracing taken from it showing the 'breakdown' of the design into the sections that will be sawn for the inlay

208

209

210

211

208. Rocks and 'slices' of hardstones, sawn to the subtle thickness necessary for the inlay sections

209. The paper 'mask' of the section to be cut, glued onto the slice of chosen stone, around the zone with the chromatic tonality desired

210. The stone is cut manually, through the joint action of a bowsaw and abrasive powders

211. Temporary anchor on the back of inlay sections

from numerous hardstone 'slices' that less expert craftsmen had sawn from the rocks (ill. 208). The master had to find the best patterns and colours for the composition in order to achieve the effects of light, shadow, 'softness' and plasticity that were so crucial to Florentine inlay-work, and the reason why it was purposefully praised as 'painting in stone'.

Individual paper sections could also be copied from the tracing and were then pasted, as cartoons, onto the slice of chosen stone, which had already been reduced to the desired thickness for the inlay and which could vary from 2 to 4 millimetres (ill. 209). The sections were cut with a bowsaw and if they were especially small, or if the stone displayed some fissure, the 'slice' was lined with a thin slab of slate. This measure avoided the risk of cracking while it was being

worked, since hardstones are resistant to engraving but fragile and easy to break. The lining applied to individual sections was then maintained even in the final assembly and overall lining of the entire intarsia (ills. 212 & 213).

Then, as today, tools of elemental simplicity were employed to cut the sections, trusting in the extraordinary dexterity of the artisans. A clamp fixed to a wooden workbench held the slice quite firmly in a vertical position (ill. 210), while the craftsman proceeded with the cutting, using a curved branch of chestnut strung with a wire of soft iron as a saw. Every movement of the saw coincided with the passage of a metal spatula gripped by the artisan's other hand, and loaded with *smeriglio* (emery), or a damp abrasive (nowadays a synthetic product, but at one time river-bed sand rich in

212 & 213. Inlay sections already cut, assembled and lined with slate

214 & 215. The ground in black Belgian marble is cut in its turn to allow a perfect fit with the inlay sections

216. The natural rosin-and-wax glue that is applied hot with a spatula, to make the inlay sections adhere to each other and the lining

217. The inlay inserted into a slab of black marble, but awaiting its final polishing

218. Small block of chalcedony and sheet of lead, used in succession to drag the abrasive powders across the inlay and thus achieve its polish

quartz). The combined action of the wire and the abrasive allowed the stone to be sawn to a pre-established profile (thanks to the sure hand of the artisan guiding the saw) and proceeded at a slow rate, the speed being determined by the hardness of the stone. The same system was used to saw the backing slab, wherever this was to remain in view, cutting it to allow a perfect fit with the inlaid image (ills. 215 & 216). In the case of the backing slab, in order to maintain it whole and make the cut only where the image would be inserted, a metal drill and an abrasive were used to make a hole in the slab so the saw-wire could pass through it and make the cut.

All section profiles had to be cut perfectly, so that in the eventual assembly the joints of these puzzles would remain virtually invisible. To this end, the thicknesses of the bow-sawn sections were further refined with metal files and abrasive powders. When the sections fitted together perfectly, work began on joining the pieces from behind, gluing groups of sections, temporarily joined with wooden or slate fillets that functioned as anchors (ill. 211). To ensure that all the sections had the same thickness, the inlay was turned onto its front and fixed to a stone slab with plaster: next the backing was levelled using large-grain abrasives dragged by spatulas, and spacers were used along the way to check that the two faces of the inlay would be perfectly parallel.

The inlay was now ready to be lined. A natural adhesive with a beeswax and rosin base (also used to join the individual pieces together) was heated and strained onto the back of the inlay, allowing the slate backing to adhere thoroughly (ill. 216). Once this support had adhered, the inlay was turned over and detached from the slab that had temporarily hidden its surface. The inlay surface was now perfectly assembled and level, but opaque because only final polishing would give the stones that luminous and durable brilliance on which so

much of their attraction depended. To this end, siliceous abrasives were repeatedly rubbed over the surface, using a finer grain each time (ill. 217). The abrasives were dampened and applied with a block of stone in the first phases and afterwards with sheets of lead (ill. 218) that, being more elastic, would hug the imperceptible surface variations, whose microporosity was gradually and totally saturated with abrasives. Thus, at the end of the entire process we see the fantastic palette of the stones light up with a reflective and intangible luminosity, the pride of Florentine inlay and the evocative response to the dreams of perpetuity that had inspired their patrons and artisans.

219. The finished inlay

Bibliography

Acidini Luchinat C., 'L'altar maggiore', in *La chiesa e il convento di Santo Spirito a Firenze* (ed. Cristina Acidini Luchinat), Florence, 1996, pp. 337-56

Acidini Luchinat C., 'L'Opificio delle Pietre Dure e i Laboratori di Restauro di Firenze', in *Grandi restauri a Firenze: L'attività dell'Opificio delle Pietre Dure 1975-2000*, Florence, 2000, pp. 9-19

Acidini Luchinat C. (ed.), *Treasures of Florence: The Medici Collection, 1400-1700*, translated from the Italian *Tesori dalle collezioni medicee* by E. Leckey, Munich, 1997

Alazard J., *L'Abbé Luigi Strozzi correspondant artistique de Mazarin, de Colbert, de Louvois et de La Teulière, Contribution à l'étude des relations artistiques entre la France et l'Italie au XVIIe siècle*, Paris, Champion, 1924

Alcouffe D., *Il mobile francese dal Rinascimento al Luigi XV*, Milan, 1981

Alfter D., *Die Geschichte des Augsburger Kabinettschranks*, Augsburg, 1986

Andaloro M. (ed.), *Federico e la Sicilia dalla terra alla corona: Arti figurative e suntuarie*, Palermo/Syracuse, 2000

Audebert N., *Voyage d'Italie*, first edition edited by Adalberto Olivero, Rome, 1983

Bacci M. and A. Forlani Tempesti, *Mostra dei disegni di Iacopo Ligozzi*, Florence, 1961

Baglione G., *Le vite de' pittori scultori e architetti*, Rome, 1649

Baldini U., A. Giusti and A. Pampaloni Martelli, *La Cappella dei Principi e le pietre dure a Firenze*, Milan, 1979

Baldinucci F., *Notizie de' professori di disegno da Cimabue in qua*, Florence, 1681-1728 (facsimile edition: Florence, 1975)

Bertani L. and E. Nardinocchi, *I Tesori di San Lorenzo: 100 capolavori di oreficeria sacra*, Florence, 1995

Berti L., *Il Principe dello Studiolo: Francesco I de' Medici e la fine del Rinascimento fiorentino*, Florence, 1967

Bizzarrie di pietre dipinte dalle collezioni dei Medici, exhibition catalogue edited by M. Chiarini and C. Acidini (Florence, 2000-1), Cinisello Balsamo, 2000

Bukovinská B., in *Prag um 1600...*, catalogue for the exhibition in Essen, Freren, 1988, pp. 513-17

Burns H., M. Collareta and D. Gasparotto, *Valerio Belli vicentino 1468 ca.-1546*, Vicenza, 2000

Butters S. B., '"Una pietra eppure non una pietra": Pietre dure e botteghe medicee nella Firenze del Cinquecento', in *La Grande Storia dell'Artigianato: Il Cinquecento*, edited by F. Franceschi and G. Fossi, Florence, 2000, pp. 133-86

Calbi E. (ed.), *Giovan Battista Dell'Era: Un artista lombardo nella Roma neoclassica*, catalogue for the exhibition in Treviglio, Milan, 2000

Chiarugi S., *Botteghe di mobilieri in Toscana, 1780-1900*, Florence, 1994

Claussen P. C., 'Marmi antichi nel medioevo romano: L'arte dei Cosmati', in *Marmi antichi* edited by G. Borghini, Rome, 1989, pp. 65-80

Colle E. (ed.), *I mobili di Palazzo Pitti: Il periodo dei Medici, 1537-1737*, Florence, 1997

Colle E., 'Pietre dure e scagliola', in *La grande storia dell'artigianato: L'Ottocento*, edited by M. Bossi and G. Gentilini, Florence, 2001, pp. 229-34

Colle E., 'Maria Luisa di Borbone e la Galleria dei Lavori in Pietre Dure di Firenze', in *DecArt*, 2003, pp. 5-14

Conigliello L., 'Alcune note su Iacopo Ligozzi e sui dipinti del 1594', in *Paragone*, 485, 1990, pp. 21-42

Cresti C., 'La Cappella dei Principi: Un Pantheon foderato di pietre dure', in *Splendori di pietre dure*, exhibition catalogue edited by A. Giusti, Florence, 1988, pp. 62-73

Curiosità di una reggia, exhibition catalogue edited by C. Piacenti and S. Pinto, Florence, 1979

Davillier J. C., *Le cabinet du duc d'Aumont et les amateurs de son temps*, Paris, Aubry, 1870

De Boodt A., *Gemmarum et lapidarum historia*, Hanau (Hesse), 1609

Di Castro A., 'Rivestimenti e tarsie marmoree a Roma fra il Cinquecento e il Seicento', in *Marmorari e argentieri a Roma e nel Lazio tra Cinquecento e Seicento*, Rome, 1994

Die Kunst des Steinschnitts: Prunkgefäße, Kameen und Commessi aus der Kunstkammer, exhibition catalogue edited by R. Distelberger, Vienna, 2002

Distelberger R., 'Dyonisio und Ferdinando Eusebio Miseroni', in *Jahrbuch der Kunsthistorischen Sammlungen in Wien*, XXXIX, 75, 1979, pp. 79-152

Distelberger R., 'Pierres précieuses du Liechtenstein', in *Connaissance des Arts*, 343, 1980, pp. 61-67

Distelberger R., 'Nuove ricerche sulla biografia dei fratelli Gasparo e Girolamo Miseroni', in *Firenze e la Toscana dei Medici nell'Europa del Cinquecento*, Congress Proceedings, III, Florence, 1983, pp. 877-84

Distelberger R., 'Archivnotizen zur Familie Miseroni in Mailand', in *Jahrbuch der Kunsthistorischen Sammlungen in Wien*, 1, 1999, pp. 310-14

Distelberger R. (ed.), *Die Kunst des Steinschnitts: Prunkgefäße, Kameen und Commessi aus der Kunstkammer*, Vienna, 2002

Evelyn J., *The diary of John Evelyn*, edited by E. S. de Beer, 2 vols, Oxford, 1955

Fischer W., *Kaiser Rudolph II: Mineraliensammler und Mäzen der Edelsteinbearbeitung*, special edition of *Der Aufschluss*, 22.1.1971

Fock C. W., 'Der Goldschmied Jacques Bylivelt aus Delft und sein Wirken in der Mediceischen Hofwerkstatt in Florenz', in *Jahrbuch der Kunsthistorischen Sammlungen in Wien*, 1974, 70, pp. 89-178

Fock C. W., 'Pietre Dure Work at the Court of Prague: Some Relations with Florence', in *Leids Kunsthistorisch Jaarboek*, 1982, I, pp. 259-69

Fock C. W., 'Pietre Dure Work at the Court of Prague and Florence: Some Relations', in *Prag um 1600...*, catalogue for the exhibition in Essen, Freren, 1988, pp. 51-58

Giacomini L., *Oratione de le Lodi di Francesco Medici*, Florence, 1587

Ginori Lisci L., *La porcellana di Doccia*, Florence, 1963

Giulianelli A. P., *Memorie degli intagliatori moderni in pietre dure, cammei e gioie dal secolo XV al secolo XVIII*, Livorno, 1753

Giuliano A., *I cammei della collezione medicea nel Museo Archeologico di Firenze*, Rome, 1989

Giusti A., P. Mazzoni and A. Pampaloni Martelli, *Il Museo dell'Opificio delle Pietre Dure a Firenze*, Milan, 1978

Giusti A., in *La Cappella dei Principi e le pietre dure a Firenze*, Milan, 1979

Giusti A., *Tesori di pietre dure a Firenze*, Milan, 1989

Giusti A., *Pietre Dure: Hardstone in Furniture and Decorations*, London, 1992

Giusti A., 'Un manoscritto inedito del XVIII secolo sulla lavorazione delle pietre dure', in *OPD Restauro*, 1992, pp.180-88

Giusti A., in *The Baptistery of San Giovanni Florence*, edited by A. Paolucci, 2 vols, Modena, 1994

Giusti A., in *Treasures of Florence: The Medici Collection, 1400-1700*, Munich, 1997

Giusti A., *Un dorato crepuscolo: Il regno di Cosimo III*, pp. 173-95

Giusti A., 'I marmi della Confessione e la tradizione del "commesso" romano', in *La Confessione nella Basilica di San Pietro in Vaticano*, edited by A. M. Pergolizzi, Rome, 2000, pp. 72-87

Giusti A., 'I fasti delle pietre dure', in *La grande storia dell'artigianato: Il Seicento e il Settecento*, edited by R. Spinelli, Florence, 2002, pp. 37-57

Giusti A., 'Origine e splendori delle botteghe granducali', in *L'ombra del genio: Michelangelo e l'arte a Firenze 1537-1631*, exhibition catalogue, Florence, 2002, pp. 115-21

Giusti A., 'Le opere e i giochi: Giuseppe Zocchi', in *FMR*, no. 156

Giusti A. (ed.), *Eternità e nobiltà di material: Itinerario artistico fra le pietre policrome*, Florence, 2003

Giusti A., *Da Roma a Firenze: Gli esordi del commesso rinascimentale*, pp. 197-230

Giusti A., *Da Firenze all'Europa: I fasti delle pietre dure*, pp. 231-70

Gnoli R., *Marmora romana*, Rome, 1988

Gnoli R. and A. Sironi (eds), *Istoria delle Pietre di Agostino del Riccio*, Turin, 1996

González-Palacios A., 'Un' autobiografia del Ghinghi', in *Antologia di Belle Arti*, 1977, 3, pp. 271-81

González-Palacios A., 'Il Laboratorio delle Pietre Dure dal 1737 al 1805', in *Le arti figurative a Napoli nel Settecento*, Naples, 1979, pp. 77-151

González-Palacios A., 'Il Real Laboratorio delle Pietre Dure', in *Civiltà del Settecento a Napoli*, exhibition catalogue, Florence, 1980, pp. 178-86

González-Palacios A., *Mosaici e pietre dure*, 2 vols, Milan, 1981

González-Palacios A., *Il tempio del Gusto: Le arti decorative in Italia fra classicismi e barocco. Roma e il regno delle Due Sicilie*, 2 vols, Milan, 1984

González-Palacios A., *Il tempio del Gusto: Le arti decorative in Italia fra classicismi e barocco. Il Granducato di Toscana e gli Stati settentrionali*, 2 vols, Milan, 1986

González-Palacios A., 'Il laboratorio del Buen Retiro a Madrid', in *Splendori di pietre dure*, exhibition catalogue, edited by A. Giusti, Florence, 1988, pp. 260-66

González-Palacios A., *Itinerario da Roma a Firenze*, Florence, 1988, pp. 43-52

González-Palacios A., *La manifattura di Luigi XIV ai Gobelins*, Florence, 1988, pp. 242-45

González-Palacios A., *Specchio dell'arte del secolo meraviglia: Viaggiatori e pietre dure a Firenze*, Florence, 1988, pp. 24-42

González-Palacios A., *The Badminton Cabinet*, London (Christie's), 1990

González-Palacios A., *Il Gusto dei Principi*, 2 vols, Milan, 1993

González-Palacios A., *Las collecciones reales españolas de mosaicos y piedras duras*, Madrid, 2001

Gregori M. (ed.), *La Natura Morta Italiana da Caravaggio al Settecento*, exhibition catalogue, Milan, 2003

Guidobaldi F., '"Sectilia pavimenta" e "incrustationes": I rivestimenti policromi pavimentali e parietali in marmo e materiali litici e litoidi dell'antichità romana', in *Eternità e nobiltà di material: Itinerario artistico fra le pietre policrome*, edited by A. Giusti, Florence, 2003, pp. 15-75

Gussoni A., 'Relazione dello Stato di Firenze', in E. Alberi, *Relazione degli ambasciatori veneti al Senato*, Florence, series II, 1841, pp. 353f.

Hahnloser H. R. and S. Brugger-Koch, *Corpus der Hartsteinschliffe des 12.-15. Jahrhunderts*, Berlin, 1985

Heikamp D., 'Reisemöbel aus dem Umkreis Philip Heinhofers', in *Anzeiger des Germanischen Nationalmuseums*, 1966, pp. 91-102

Heikamp D., *Il Tesoro di Lorenzo il Magnifico: I vasi*, II, Florence, 1972

Heikamp D., 'Opere di commesso di pietre dure a Praga', in *Splendori di pietre dure…*, exhibition catalogue, Florence, 1988, pp. 232-37

I marmi colorati della Roma Imperiale, exhibition catalogue by P. Pensabene and L. Lazzarini (Rome, 2002-3), edited by M. De Nuccio and L. Ungaro, Venice, 2002

Keysler J. G., *Travels through Germany, Bohemia, Hungary, Switzerland, Italy and Lorraine….*, London, 1756-57

Koch E., *Shah Jahan and Orpheus: The Pietre Dure Decoration and the Programme of the Throne in the Hall of Public Audiences at the Red Fort of Delhi*, Graz, 1988

Krcálová J. and C. Aschengreen Piacenti, category 'Castrucci', in *Dizionario Biografico degli Italiani*, 22, Rome, 1979

Kriegbaum F., 'Dokumente über künstlerische Beziehungen Augsburgs zum Medizeischen Hof in Spätrenaissance', in *Mitteilungen des Kunsthistorischen Institutes in Florenz*, V, 1939, pp. 203-8

Kris E., *Meister und Meisterwerke der Steinschneidenkunst in der Italienischen Renaissance*, 2 vols, Vienna, 1929

L'ombra del Genio: Michelangelo e l'arte a Firenze 1537-1631, exhibition catalogue edited by M. Chiarini, A. P. Darr and C. Giannini (Florence/Chicago/Detroit 2002-3), Milan, 2002

Magnificenza alla corte dei Medici: Arte a Firenze alla fine del Cinquecento, exhibition catalogue edited by M. Gregori and D. Heikamp (Florence, 1997-98), Milan, 1997

Marmi antichi, edited by G. Borghini, Rome, 1989

Massinelli A. M., *Hardstones (The Gilbert Collection)*, London, 2000

Morrogh A. (ed.), *Disegni di architetti fiorentini 1540-1640*, Florence, 1985

Napoleone C. (ed.), *Delle Pietre Antiche: Il trattato sui marmi romani di Faustino Corsi*, Milan, 2001

Neumann E., 'Florentiner Mosaik aus Prag', in *Jahrbuch der Kunsthistorischen Sammlungen in Wien*, VII, 53, 1957, pp. 75-158

Norcini C., *La produzione dell'Opificio delle Pietre Dure dall'Unità d'Italia agli anni Ottanta dell'Ottocento*, thesis, Università degli Studi di Siena, Siena, 2002-3

Pampaloni Martelli A., 'Edoardo Marchionni: La trasformazione dell'Opificio delle Pietre Dure in Laboratorio di restauro', in *Studi di storia dell'arte in onore di Ugo Procacci*, II, Milan, 1977, pp. 360-66

Pampaloni Martelli A., in *La Cappella dei Principi e le pietre dure a Firenze*, Milan, 1979

Paris 1400: Les arts sous Charles VI, catalogue for exhibition at the Louvre, Paris, 2004

Parker J., *Decorative Art from the Samuel H. Kress Collection at the Metropolitan Museum of Art*, London, 1964

Pelli G., *Serie di ritratti di uomini illustri toscani*, Florence, 1766-73

Pensabene P. (ed.), *Marmi antichi II: Cave e tecnica di lavorazione. Provenienze e distribuzione*, Rome, 1998

Peroni A. (ed.), *Il Duomo di Pisa*, Vol. 2, Modena, 1995

Prag um 1600: Kunst und Kultur am Hofe Rudolfs II, catalogue for the exhibition in Essen, Freren, 1988

Przyborowski C., *Die Ausstattung der Fürstenkapelle an der Basilika von San Lorenzo in Florenz: Versuch einer Rekonstruktion*, thesis (1980), 2 vols, Berlin, 1982

Przyborowski C., 'Commesso-Tafeln im Florentiner Kabinett, Schloß Favorite bei Rastatt: Studien zur Arbeiten der Galleria dei Lavori in Florenz zu Beginn des 18. Jahrhunderts', in *Mitteilungen des Kunsthistorischen Institutes in Florenz*, 42, 1998, pp. 383-457

Raggio O., 'The Farnese table: A rediscovered work of Vignola', in *The Metropolitan Museum of Art Bulletin*, XVIII, March 1960, pp. 213-31

Riccardi-Cubitt M., *The Art of the Cabinet*, London, 1992

Rossi F., *La pittura di pietra*, Florence, 1967

Samoyault-Verlet C. and J.-P., *Château de Fontainebleau: Musée Napoléon Ier, Napoléon et la famille impériale, 1804-1815*, Paris, 1986

Santi B., *Il pavimento del Duomo di Siena*, Siena, 1982

Saule B., 'Précisions sur la grande table en marqueterie de pierres dures du Muséum d'Histoire Naturelle de Paris', in *Revue de gemmologie*, 73, 1982, pp. 2-4

Scalini M., in *Treasures of Florence: The Medici Collection 1400-1700*, Munich, 1997

Setterwall A., 'Some Louis Seize Furniture Decorated with Pietra Dura Reliefs', in *The Burlington Magazine*, CI, 1959, 681, pp. 425-35

Spinosa N., 'Ancora sul Laboratorio di pietre dure e sull'Arazzeria; i documenti dell'Accademia di Belle Arti a Napoli', in *Le arti figurative a Napoli nel Settecento*, Naples, 1979, pp. 325-84

Splendori di pietre dure: Arte di corte nella Firenze dei Granduchi, exhibition catalogue edited by A. Giusti, Florence, 1988

Terry A., 'Opus sectile in the Eufrasius Cathedral at Porec', in *Dumbarton Oaks Papers*, 40, 1986, pp. 147-64

Tesouros Reais: Palacio Nacional da Ajuda, Lisbon, 1992

Tondo L. and F. M. Vanni, *Le gemme dei Medici e dei Lorena nel Museo Archeologico di Firenze*, Florence, 1990

Tosi A., *Inventare la realtà: Giuseppe Zocchi e la Toscana del Settecento*, Florence, 1997

Tuena F., 'Appunti per la storia del commesso romano: Il "Franciosino maestro di tavole e il cardinale Giovanni Ricci"', in *Antologia di Belle Arti*, 1988, 33-34, pp. 54-69

Tuena F., 'I marmi commessi del tardo Rinascimento romano', in *Marmi antichi* edited by G. Borghini, Rome, 1989, pp. 80-97

Valeriani R., 'Il Real Laboratorio delle Pietre Dure di Napoli', in *Splendori di pietre dure...*, Florence, 1988, pp. 250-59

Vasari G., *Le Vite de' più eccellenti pittori, scultori e architettori*, Florence, 1568, new edition edited by G. Previtali, Milan, 1962-66

Villa Medici: Il sogno di un cardinale. Collezioni e artisti di Ferdinando de' Medici, exhibition catalogue edited by M. Hochmann, Rome, 1999

Vincent C., in *Liechtenstein: The Princely Collections*, exhibition catalogue, New York, 1985, pp. 42-55

Zobi A., *Notizie storiche sull'origine e progressi dei lavori di commesso in pietre dure che si eseguiscono nell'I. e R. Stabilimento di Firenze (1837)*, second edition, Florence, 1853

Index

Figures in *italic* refer to illustrations

Adam, Robert 231–2, 232
Alberti, Leon Battista 19, 22
Alessandrino, Cardinal (Michele Bonelli) 29–31
Altoviti, Bindo 27, 28
Ammannati, Bartolommeo 25
Andrew III of Hungary 15
Anjou, Duke of 16
Audebert, Nicolas 54
Aumont, Ducque d' 208–11

Baglione, Giovanni 31
Baldinucci, Filippo 75, 84–88
Barberini, Cardinal Antonio 88
Barone, Francesco di 26
Baumgartner, Melchior 144
Baumhauer, Joseph 208, 211
Bay, Filippo 44
Beaufort, Duke of 103
Belli, Valerio 34
Benotti, Domenico 235
Benzi, Massimiliano Soldani 95
Bernini, Gian Lorenzo 44
Berry, Jean de 16
Betti, Francesco 235
Betti, Niccolò 232, 240, 242, 244
Bianchini, Gaetano 235
Bianco, Baccio del 84, 100–1
Bijlivert, Jacques 51, 54
Bilivert, Giovanni 75, 76, 77
Bimbi, Bartolomeo 181
Boel, Pieter 155
Bonaparte, Elisa 214–16, 215, 219
Bonaparte, Joseph 219
Bonelli, Michele, *see* Alessandrino, Cardinal
Boodt, Anselmus Boetius de 115–16, 135
Borghese, Francesco 160
Bosch, Philipp van den 122
Bosi, Enrico 236
Branchi, Filippo 150
Bril, Paul 123
Bruch, Ranier 34
Bruni, Riccardo 95
Buffon, Georges-Louis Leclerc de 208
Buoninsegni brothers 235–36
Buontalenti, Bernardo 50, 51, 54

Cacialli, Giuseppe 223
Calderón, Don Rodrigo 42
Cambio, Arnolfo di 13
Cameron, Robert 173
Cappella, Gennaro 196
Carli, Pietro 38
Carlieri, Carlo 214, 216, 222

Carlin, Martin 210, 211
Caroni, Ambrogio 52, 68, 75, 111, 116
Caroni, Stefano 52, 64, 68, 75, 111
Carracci, Annibale 35
Carrey, Jacques 155
Castrucci, Cosimo 112–13, 117–23, 135
Castrucci, Cosimo II 128
Castrucci, Giovanni 115, 118–19, 120, 122, 126, 128, 131
Catherine II, Empress of Russia 173
Ceci, Giacomo 189, 192
Charles I of Liechtenstein 117, 131
Charles III of Bourbon (Carlos III, King of Spain) 103, 188–89, 196, 202
Charles IV of Bohemia 15
Charles IV of Bourbon 203
Charles V 16
Charles XIII, King of Sweden 211
Cheller, Jean 34
Chilolz, Remis 34
Cigoli, Lodovico 73, 75
Cioci, Antonio 184–85, 187, 189, 190–91, 214, 216, 219, 236
Clement VIII, Pope 34, 35
Conti Guidi, Bishop Francesco dei 187
Corniole, Giovanni delle 18, 49
Cosmati family 13
Cotte, Robert de 155
Cozzarelli, Guidoccio 18
Cremona, Giacomo Antonio 34
Cromwell, Oliver 88, 94
Cucci, Domenico 152

Da Vinci, Leonardo 83
Daguerre, Dominique 211
Dell'Era, Giovan Battista 187, 192
Demidoff, Prince Anatoly 232, 236
Desiderius, Abbot 13
Desiderius, King 14
Dolci, Carlo 98
Don Juan of Austria 42
Donatello 18
Donato, Maestro 31
Donnini, Gaspare 196
Dosio, Giovanni Antonio 26, 42, 43
Dupré, Giovanni 227

Emanuele the German 120
Eusebius, Ferdinand 115
Evelyn, John 235

Falck, Jonas 83
Farnese, Cardinal Alessandro 24–25, 26
Ferdinand III, Emperor 115
Ferdinand III of Habsburg-Lorraine 216, 222–23, 236
Ferroni, Giovan Battista 202, 203
Ferrucci, Francesco 68
Fiammingo, Ermanno 34

Fiammingo, Giovanni (Giovanni degli Studioli) 36
Fiesole, Ludovico da 26
Flach, Iacopo (Jakob) di Ian 68
Flippart, Charles-Joseph 202–3, 203
Foggini, Giovanni Battista 82, 95, 98–99, 102, 160, 170
Fontana, Annibale 48
Fontana, Domenico 35
Francis I, King of France 150
Francis I, King of the Two Sicilies 219
Francis Stephen of Lorraine 167, 170, 202
Frederick Augustus of Saxony 164
Frederick II, the Great, King of Prussia 15, 202
Frederick IV, King of Denmark 164

Gaffurri, Cristofano 64, 68, 75, 111
Gaffurri, Giorgio 52
George IV, King of Great Britain 211
Ghiberti, Lorenzo 18
Ghinghi, Francesco 103, 164, 167, 188, 189
Giachetti, Gian Ambrogio 150, 211
Giorgi, Giovan Battista 219, 222, 224, 225, 227, 228–30, 232, 240
Giorgi, Tito 227
Gregory XIII, Pope 35

Hamilton, Duke of 231
Heinhofer, Philip 136, 143–44
Henry II, Emperor 14
Henry IV, King of France 136, 150
Hertel, Hans G. 127
Hoare, Henry, II 28
Homer 9
Hume, Robert 232, 233

Jannitzer, Wenzel 135
Johann Wilhelm, Elector 99
John, St 9
Julius III, Pope 25

Karl, Landgrave of Hesse-Kassel 142, 146
Karl Eusebius of Liechtenstein 135
Kilian, Lukas 127

Leo XIII, Pope 242
Leopold I, Emperor 115
Leopold II, Grand Duke 233
Leopold III, Grand Duke 227–30
Lignereux, Martin-Eloy 211
Ligozzi, Jacopo 56–57, 59, 59, 68, 76, 78–79, 80, 81, 83, 84, 233
Longhi, Pietro 203
Louis XIV, King of France 44, 47, 94, 150–56, 211
Louis XVI, King of France 152
Ludwig II of Bavaria 242

Maderno, Carlo 35
Mann, Sir Horace 202

Manzoni, Alessandro 237
Marcellini, Carlo 95
Marchionni, Edoardo 240, 242–43, 250, 251
Margaret of Savoy 237
Maria Luisa of Bourbon 213–14, 219
Maria Maddalena of Austria 83
Maria Pia of Savoy 236
Maria Theresa, Empress of Austria 170
Marie Antoinette 208
Masnago, Alessandro 111
Mazarin, Cardinal 44, 150, 152
Medici, Catherine de' 26, 150
Medici, Cosimo de', the Elder 18, 18
Medici, Cosimo I de' 22, 28, 34, 42, 47, 49–50, 50
Medici, Cosimo II de' 35, 64, 75–76, 83, 136, 146
Medici, Cosimo III de' 94–95, 98–99, 102–3, 128, 146, 159, 164, 170
Medici, Ferdinando I de' 28, 36, 37, 42–43, 44, 46, 47, 47, 53, 54, 64, 68, 75, 84, 109, 111, 116, 150, 167, 170, 187, 222, 223
Medici, Ferdinando II de' 83–84, 88, 94, 135, 136, 144, 211, 233
Medici, Francesco I de' 26, 28, 42, 50–54, 59, 64, 76, 109
Medici, Gian Gastone 103, 159, 164, 171, 188
Medici, Lorenzo de', the Magnificent 16, 47, 49, 50
Medici, Maria de' 150
Merlini, Cosimo 83
Meynard, Jean 24
Michelangelo 24
Michelozzi family 59
Michelozzo 22
Migliorini, Ferdinando 150, 152, 155
Migliorini, Orazio 150
Minardi, Giovanni 54
Miseroni, Alessandro 110
Miseroni, Aurelio 110
Miseroni, Dionisio 110, 115
Miseroni, Gasparo 48–49
Miseroni, Giovanni Ambrogio 110
Miseroni, Girolamo 48
Miseroni, Ottavio 109, 110–11, 110, 115, 118
Mola, Gaspare 34–35
Montelatici, Alfonso 242
Montelatici, Giovanni 242
Montelatici, Mario 242
Morghen, Giovanni 192
Mugnai, Francesco 102, 142, 144, 146
Mugnai, Giovanni 198, 202, 219
Murat, Caroline (née Bonaparte) 216, 219
Murat, Joachim 219

Napoleon 181, 188, 203, 216, 219
Napoletano, Filippo 36–37
Nigetti, Matteo 88
Nigra, Constantino 236
Noferi, Giovanni Antonio 196

Pandolfini, Giuliano 126, 128, 132–33, 135
Pannini, Giovanni Paolo 170
Parler, Peter 15
Partini, Ferdinando 187, 192
Paul V, Pope 35–37
Permoser, Balthasar 95
Pescia, Pier Maria Serbaldi da 22, 49
Peter Leopold of Habsburg-Lorraine 181–82, 187, 213
Pfaff, Nikolaus 110
Philip II, King of Spain 29
Philip the Bold 16
Piero the Gouty 16, 47
Piranesi 187
Pius IV, Pope 26
Pius V, Pope 25, 26
Pius IX, Pope 233
Pliny the Elder 10, 21
Poccetti, Bernardino 68–69, 76, 84, 120, 126
Poggetti, Francesco 202
Poggetti, Luigi 202
Polo, Domenico di 49
Pompadour, Marquise de 208
Ponzio, Flaminio 36
Porfirio (da Leccio), Bernardino di 28, 50
Porta, Giacomo della 35

Rega, Filippo 219
Resi, Luigi 237
Ricci, Cardinal 26
Ricci, Paolo 242, 248
Riccio, Agostino del 9, 35, 64, 116
Richelieu, Cardinal 42, 150
Rossi, Giovanni Antonio de' 34, 50
Rovere, Grand Duchess Vittoria della 160, 233
Rubens, Peter Paul 16
Rudolf II von Habsburg, Emperor 15, 64, 109–11, 115–16, 131

Sadeler, Egid 122–23
Sangallo, Guiliano da 21–22
Scacciati, Andrea 102
Scappini, F. 236, 241
Senger, Philip 95
Servi, Constantino de' 76, 118
Sibyl Augusta, Margravine of Baden-Baden 159–60, 164
Siriès, Carlo 170, 222, 223, 227
Siriès, Louis 170
Siriès, Luigi 182, 187, 214
Sixtus V, Pope 28, 30, 35
Stecchi, Domenico 202
Stella, Jacques 35
Stevens, Pieter 123
Strozzi, Abate Luigi 150, 155
Studioli, Giovanni degli (Giovanni Fiammingo) 36
Sustris, Friedrich 136

Targone, Pompeo 31
Tempesta, Antonio 164
Tiepolo, Giovan Battista 203
Torricelli, Giovan Battista 146
Torricelli, Giuseppe Antonio 98–99, 102, 103, 242

Vanni, Curzio 31
Vanvitelli, Luigi 192, 198, 219
Vasari, Giorgio 22, 27, 28, 48, 50, 54
Vermeyen, Jan 111
Vernet, Joseph 170
Verrocchio, Andrea del 18, 18, 22
Vianen, Paulus van 110
Victor Emmanuel II of Savoy 236, 237
Vignola, Jacopo 24–25, 26
Vinne, Leonard van der 94, 95
Volterra, Francesco da 35
Vries, Adriaen de 110

Wagner, Giuseppe 202–3
Wechter, Johannes 122
Weisweiler, Adam 155, 156, 211, 211, 231
Wittel, Gaspar van 203

Zobi 135, 182, 227
Zocchi, Giuseppe 170, 172, 173, 173, 176, 177, 181, 182, 183, 186, 202–3
Zumbo, Gaetano 98

Picture Credits

© archives OPD, Florence, with the following exceptions:
RMN ills. I, 121–23, 126, 149, 164–67; Joseph Martin II, 9, 157–60, 162, 163; Roberto Ponzani/Archivio FMR, Villanova di Castenaso III, 88, 113–15; Scala 1, 4, 12; Erich Lessing/AKG 2, 11, 96; Kunsthistorisches Museum, Vienna 3, 76, 89, 91–95, 137; Rabatti & Domingie, Florence 5, 6, 13, 14, 184, 185; Bibliothèque Nationale de France, Paris 7; Ferrante Ferranti 10, 25, 32; J.P. Getty Museum, Los Angeles 15, 52; Giovanni Dagli Orti 16; The Metropolitan Museum of Art, Harris Brisbane Dick Fund, New York 19; Vladimir Terebenin/Hermitage Museum, Saint Petersburg 21, 147, 154, 190, 191; Stourhead House, Wiltshire 22; Prado Museum, Madrid 24, 101; John Gibbons Studios/All Souls College, Oxford 27; National Museums, Liverpool 28; Chuzeville brothers/RMN 35; Soprintendenza Archeologica, Rome 53; Bayerisches Nationalmuseum, Munich 63, 78; Image Art, Antibes 64, 71; Rosenborg Castle, Copenhagen 66, 67, 117; Residenz, Munich 70, 103; Cromwell Museum, Huntington 74; H. Maertens/Staatliches Museum, Schwerin 77; Bayerische Verwaltung der Staatlichen Schlösser, Gärten und Seen, Öffentlichkeitsarbeit, Munich 86, 87; AKG images 98; Musée des Beaux-Arts du Canada, Ottawa 99; Landesmuseum, Kassel 116; Muséum National d'Histoire Naturelle, Paris 118; Arnaudet/RMN 125; Alexis Daflos/Kungliga Slottet, Stockholm 128; Landesmedienzentrum Baden-Württemberg, Stuttgart 129, 134–36; Thomas Goldschmidt/Badisches Landesmuseum, Karlsruhe 130; Schlosskirche, Rastatt 131; Institute of Art, Detroit 138; Grünes Gewolbe, Dresden 139; Matthias Holfeld/Stadtmuseum, Berlin, 144; private collections 148, 198; Patrimonio Nacional, Madrid 153; Royal Collection Picture Library ©? HM Queen Elizabeth II 168; Victoria and Albert Museum, London 170, 188; Gilbert Collection, Somerset House, London 172, 175, 189, 197; Musée Poldi-Pezzoli, Milan 176; Instituto Valencia de Don Juan, Madrid 177; Ministero per i Beni e Attività Culturali, Caserta 178; PH3-Manuel Silveira Ramos/IPAR, Lisbon 200, 203; P. Zigrossi/Pinacoteca, Vatican 202

J. Sach
Christmas 2009